Bullmastiff

A guide to selection, care, nutrition, rearing,

training, health, breeding, sports and play.

A must for both owners and people who are

interested in finding a suitable dog breed.

© 2009 About Pets bv
P.O. Box 26, 9989 ZG Warffum, the Netherlands
www.aboutpets.info
E-mail: management@aboutpets.info

ISBN: 9789058218223

First edition 2009

Photos: About Pets photography team

Acknowledgements:
Photos: fam. Mulders, Debbie Kuiper, fam. Brienissen Lene and Marcel Huls
and J. Snijders
Anatomic illustrations: Hill's
Graphs: Courtesy of Royal Canin

Contents

Foreword 6

In general 8

Purchase 18

Travelling 26

Feeding. 30

Care 45

Rearing. 52

Breeding 72

Sports and shows. 78

Parasites. 84

Health 86

First aid for dogs 96

More danger. 114

Tips. 120

Internet 122

Addresses. 126

Profile 128

Foreword

The book you are holding is a basic 'owner's manual' for everyone owning a Bullmastiff and also for those who are considering buying a Bullmastiff. What we have done in this book is to give the basic information to help the future owner of a Bullmastiff look after his or her pet responsibly. Too many people still buy a pet before really understanding what they are about to get into.

This book goes into the broad history of the Bullmastiff, the breed standard and some pros and cons of buying a Bullmastiff. You will also find essential information on feeding, initial training and an introduction to reproduction. Finally we pay attention to day-by-day care, health and some breed-specific ailments.

Based on this information, you can buy a Bullmastiff, having thought it through carefully, and keep it as a pet in a responsible manner. A properly brought-up and well-trained dog is more than just a dog. Invest a little extra in a puppy training course or an obedience course. There are also excellent books available that go deeper into certain aspects than is possible here.

About Pets

In general

The Bullmastiff is one of the biggest breeds that we know. This big and special dog is highly intelligent, obedient, but also independent and powerful.

It is kind and gentle and sometimes it can behave very affectionately. Every Bullmastiff has its own personality. Obedience always is very important, for the dogs belonging to the big breeds, such as the Bullmastiff, obedience is extremely important.

We never should treat the Bullmastiff as we do other guard dogs. In the old days, the ancestors of the Bullmastiffs always had to take their own decisions regarding keeping the intruder under control without biting hard. The Bullmastiff needs to be brought up with discipline, very consistently and above all very affectionately. This is not difficult, because the Bullmastiff's nature is to be obedient. In most cases a Bullmastiff will outperform all participants in its group during a 'Behaviour and Obedience' course. As it is a working dog, it likes to be kept busy.

Origins

Thousands of years ago, the Tibetan Dog was living in Tibet. Today we still know of the Tibetan Mastiff as an extremely big dog. The primitive Tibetan dog could maintain without any changes because of the isolated mountain scenery.

Marco Polo got to know these big dogs, which he described as "as big as a donkey", during his visit to the Great Mogol. The Sumerian people took these big dogs with them from the Tibetan Highlands during their emigrations around 3800 BC. They settled between Tigris and the Euphrates.

The Greeks called this territory Mesopotamia, "the land between two rivers".

When Alexander the Great, 350 BC, entered into combat with the Medes and Persians, he met an army that was equipped with fighting dogs. The dogs that were captured, mastiff like dogs, were taken to Greece of course.

The Phoenicians (originated from today's Lebanon) were trading with the present Europe. In that way the dogs of the Sumerians finally arrived at our coastal regions.

The Greek empire declined and the Romans conquered it. Their fighting dogs had to work in the amphitheatres and had to join the Roman legions. The cattle that the Romans took with them had to be herded by these dogs as well.

Once the road was cleared and settlements were founded, colonists and traders arrived and they also were accompanied by their own dogs.
Of course the dogs that had to guard the toll roads were eventually left behind and on the way dogs were possibly exchanged or strayed away from the Roman legions and stayed behind. Some mountain dogs could have descended from these dogs, such as the Bernese Mountain Dog, the St Bernard and the Rottweiler. Especially when the Roman legions moved back, many dogs were left behind. The Rottweiler has certainly developed from these dogs.
The Indo-Germanic people took Mastiff-like dogs with them from the Far East.

In the end it were the Englishmen that have imported many dogs as a consequence of being a maritime country and a colonial power.
Meanwhile the Molosser is an extinct breed. It is regarded as the ancestor of today's English Mastiff Dog, the Dogue the Bordeaux, Neapolitan Mastiff and the Bullmastiff.

History

As long ago as 1785, there was written reference to large dogs of the Bullmastiff kind. These dogs had various names including the Keepers Night dog, Mastiff with a dash of Bullmastiff and Large Bullmastiff. These dogs were mostly working dogs and there was evidence that these dogs were not only the Mastiff and the Bullmastiff. They also used the Great Dane, the St Bernard, the Bloodhounds and the Dogue de Bordeaux.

The name Bullmastiff is a combination of the names of the breeds it originated from. Its ancestors are the Bulldog and the Mastiff, both of which originated from Great Britain. The first crossbreeds date from several hundred years ago. The Bulldog was crossed in because of its speed and its temperament and the Mastiff because of its size and power. From the Bulldogs, the brindled coat and the shape of the head were passed on to these first crossbreeds. The shape of the head was necessary to allow the dog to continue breathing while it had to hold onto somebody or something. The Bullmastiff contains about 60 % Mastiff and 40 % Bulldog.

The breeders in Great Britain kept on selecting these dogs and some written statements can still be found about this.

'Out of the crossbreed Mastiff and Bulldog derived a dog that was substantially bigger than the Mastiff' according to the opinion of the French author Bufon. The English author Stonehenge also wrote about these crossbreeds and in 1871 Hutchinson reports about the nature of these dogs. He praises them for their excellent trainabilities.

In the old days, the Bulldog was used by gamekeepers, but these were dogs that liked to bite and sometimes the poachers were killed before they were able to go to court and before they were hanged. The dog that derived from the crossbreeds had an advantage because of its dark colour, it had excellent stamina and it was able to catch off a poacher and to guard him until the gamekeeper arrived. Killing is not in its blood.

Mostly gamekeepers used this breed. The Police also found the Bullmastiff invaluable and used them as a guard in warehouses and the dockland areas. By using the St Bernhard, the Great Dane and the Newfoundland for crossbreeding, some less successful breeding results came into being. There was an attempt to breed a long haired variety, but there was not much interest in these new breeds.

Selective breeding made this dog to what it is nowadays. Mr. Sam Mosely from the Farcroft kennels used to be an important breeder in the old days. His dogs were sold all over the world. The breed standard still had to be drafted. They wanted to preserve the character and sometimes the puppies looked more like one of the ancestors and sometimes like the other one.

The Bullmastiff was recognised as a pure breed by the Kennel Club in 1924 and dogs were registered in the studbook. However, this could only be done if the dogs had three generations of ancestors that were Bullmastiffs, and thus were purebred. In 1925 the National Bullmastiff Police-dog Club was established, and Mr. Mosely became the first President.

Mr S E Moseley is seen as the father of the breed and all Bullmastiffs today would be able to trace their pedigrees back to his Farcroft kennels. In 1925 Farcroft Fidelity (born in 1921) was the first to win a first prize at a show held under Kennel Club rules and the first to qualify for registration in the Kennel Club Stud Book. The first Bullmastiff Champion was a Brindle bitch, Farcroft Silvo (born on 18/3/25). One of the most influential stud dogs was Ch Roger of the Fens (born on 7/11/29); he sired 10 UK Champions.

The American Kennel Association registered the breed in 1934.

The Bullmastiff today
Today the Bullmastiff is no longer widely used as a working guard-dog but its instincts are still there and it will guard its family with all its considerable strength if it needs to do so. Trained and socialised, the Bullmastiff will make a wonderful family pet and guardian.

Character
A dog's character is generally determined by the tasks it was bred for. At the beginning of the 20th century the English legislation concerning poaching was extremely tight. During times of dire poverty, people were often forced to go poaching. Gamekeepers therefore needed to have a dog that was obedient and could take its own decisions when necessary. As the forest was their working-area, an agile dog was desirable, as well as a dog with power. The Bullmastiff also was called 'night-dog', the Keepers Night Dog, i.e. belonging to the gamekeeper. In those days the gamekeeper mainly used to live in the middle of the forests together with his dog.

As far as its work was concerned, the Bullmastiff of the gamekeeper certainly was allowed to be somewhat aggressive. Another name for the Bullmastiff was 'Holding-Dog' because of its ability to keep hold of the poachers. Due to a change in the social circumstances, the Bullmastiff became more and more a companion. It remained an excellent guard-dog, which is never afraid. When necessary, it will protect its family.

Most of the time, the Bullmastiff does not even need to take action, because it has quite an impressive appearance and burglars usually run away as fast as they can.

The Bullmastiff is sensitive to the human voice, it is extremely intelligent and therefore it can be trained very well. It does not like being told off, but it really appreciates an enthusiastic 'Well done'. The Bullmastiff has a very special character, because it can be so extremely gentle and full of love, intelligent, active and strong, but it can also be very protective and then its hidden strength will be shown.

UK Kennel Club and its breed standards
What does the UK Kennel Club do?
To say it in their own words: "The Kennel Club is committed to developing and supporting a nation of responsible dog owners. As well as organising events and campaigns to help dog owners meet their responsibilities, the Kennel Club also produces a range of literature to assist the dog owning public."
What is the use of a Breed Standard?
The Kennel Club's answer: "The basis of breed shows is the judging of dogs against the 'Breed Standard', which is the prescribed blueprint of the particular breed of dog. For all licensed breed shows, the Kennel Club Breed Standards must be used for the judging of dogs."

More about the UK Kennel Club Breed Standards:
"The Breed Standards are owned by the Kennel Club, and all changes are subject to approval by the Kennel Club General Committee. New Breed Standards, for newly recognised breeds, are drawn up once the breed has become sufficiently established within the UK. Careful research is conducted into the historical background, health and temperament of any new breed before Kennel Club recognition is granted. The Kennel Club currently recognises 196 breeds. Upon recognition, breeds are placed on the Imported Breed Register until they are deemed eligible for transferral to the Breed Register". A standard provides a guideline for breeders and judges. It is something of an ideal that dogs of each breed must strive to match. With some breeds, dogs are already being bred that match the ideal. Other breeds have a long way to go. There is a list of defects for each breed. These can be serious defects that disqualify the dog, in which case it will be excluded from breeding. Permitted defects are not serious, but do cost points in a show. A standard has been developed for all breeds recognised by the FCI (Fédération Cynologique Internationale). The FCI is the umbrella organisation of the Western European dog world. The officially approved breed associations of the member countries provide translations of the breed standard.

The UK Kennel Club Breed Standard of the Bullmastiff

British Breed Evolved From The Old English Mastiff and the Bullmastiff
Primarily used as a guard dog and, in olden times, to help the gamekeeper in the apprehension of poachers.
Naturally intelligent and observant, it is easily trained but likes to have a reason for doing things. Highly spirited, he makes a happy companion who is totally reliable both physically and mentally. Devoted to its 'family', his bravery and courage are legendary, defending them against intruders. It can quickly assess a situation and this, combined with its acute hearing, makes it an excellent housedog. It is very strong, but amenable to kindly discipline.

Characteristics
Powerful, enduring, active and reliable.

General Appearance
Powerful build, symmetrical, showing great strength, but not cumbersome; sound and active.

Temperament
High spirited, alert and faithful.

Head and skull

Skull large and square, viewed from every angle, fair wrinkle when interested, but not when in repose. Circumference of skull may equal height of dog when measured at top of shoulder; broad and deep with well filled cheeks. Pronounced stop. Muzzle short; distance from tip of nose to stop approx one third of length from tip of nose to centre of occiput, broad under eyes and sustaining nearly the same width to end of nose; blunt and cut of square, forming right angle with upper line of face, and at same time proportionate with skull. Under jaw broad to end. Nose broad with widely spreading nostrils; flat, neither pointed nor turned up in profile. Flews not pendulous, never hanging below level of lower jaw.

Eyes

Dark or hazel, of medium size, set apart the width of the muzzle with furrow between. Light or yellow eyes highly undesirable.

Ears

V shaped, folded back, set on wide and high, level of occiput giving square appearance to skull which is most important. Small and deeper in colour than body. Point of ear level with eye when alert. Rose ears are highly undesirable.

Mouth

Level desired but slightly undershot allowed but not preferred. Canine teeth large and set wide apart, other teeth strong, even and well placed.

Neck

Well arched, moderate length, very muscular and almost equal to skull in circumference.

Forequarters

Chest wide and deep, well let down between forelegs, with deep brisket. Shoulders muscular, sloping and powerful, not overloaded. Forelegs powerful and straight, well boned, set wide apart, presenting a straight front. Pasterns straight and strong.

Body

Back short and straight, giving compact carriage, but not so short as to interfere with movement. Roach and sway backs highly undesirable.

Hindquarters

Loins wide and muscular with fair depth of flank. Hind legs strong, and muscular; with well developed second thighs, denoting power and activity, not cumbersome. Hocks moderately bent. Cow hocks highly undesirable.

Feet

Well arched, cat-like, with rounded toes, pads hard. Dark toenails desirable. Splay feet highly undesirable.

Tail

Set high, strong at root and tapering, reaching to hocks, carried straight or curved, but not hound fashion. Crank tails highly undesirable.

Gait/movement

Movement indicates power and strength of purpose. When moving straight, neither front nor hind legs should cross or plait, right front and rear left legs rising and falling at the same time. A firm back line unimpaired by powerful thrust from hind legs denoting a balanced and harmonious movement.

Coat

Short and hard, weather resistant, lying flat to body. Long silky or woolly coats highly undesirable.

Colour

Any shade of brindle, fawn or red, colour to be pure and clear. A slight white marking on chest permissible. Other white markings undesirable. Black muzzle essential, toning off towards eyes, with dark markings around eyes contributing towards expression.

Size

Height at shoulder: dogs: 63.5-68.5 cm (25-27 ins); bitches 61-66 cm (24-26 ins). Weight: dogs 50-59 KGs (110-130 lbs.); bitches 41-50 KGs (90-110 lbs.).

Faults

Any departure from the forgoing points should be considered a fault and the seriousness with which the fault should be regarded should be in exact proportion to the degree of fault.

Note

Male animals should have two apparently normal testicles fully descended into the scrotum.

Last Updated - September 2000

Breed standard by courtesy of the Kennel Club of Great Britain.

Purchase

If, after careful consideration, you have decided to buy a Bullmastiff, there are a number of possibilities. Do you want a puppy or an adult dog? Should it be a male or female?
And, of course, the question arises as to where you should buy the dog. Should you buy it privately or from a reliable breeder? For your own and the animal's sake, a few things should be decided in advance. After all, you want a dog that suits your situation.

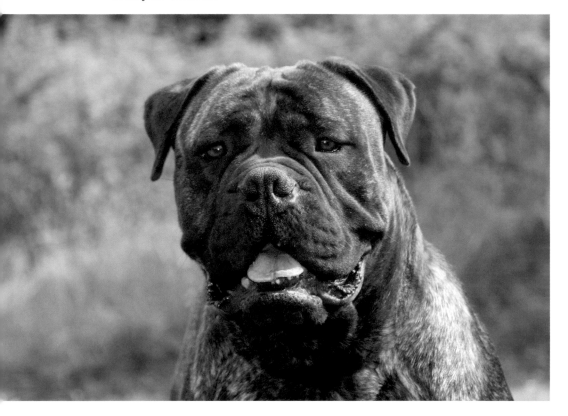

Pros and cons of the Bullmastiff

The Bullmastiff is really a faithful animal, which becomes a part of its family. The Bullmastiff is not a dog for everybody, which is why the breed-clubs have special people who inform others about this breed. To rear this dog, its owner needs to spend a lot of time on this subject. In case you think that its character is not quite what you expect from a dog, please do not buy a Bullmastiff. One is fond of this breed or does not like the breed at all, there is no middle ground.

Although the Bullmastiff can be a very active dog, it is not overly energetic. Sometimes it can look like the Bullmastiff is a lazy dog and because of that it can be kept in an apartment-building very well. Of course this has to be an apartment–building with an elevator.
Young dogs are not allowed to walk up and down the stairs and lifting up this big breed is not a pleasure, it might even be impossible.

The positive character-traits of a Bullmastiff are:
It is a good guard-dog, it is obedient, it learns fast and it is very intelligent. And of course it has a balanced character which really is a very positive trait.

When we think of negative traits, one could say that it easily becomes overweight as a result of its laziness. Sometimes it can be very dominant and for that reason it needs an experienced owner. It can try to impose its will, it has the tendency to snore and it can slaver as well. It is never wise to feed the dog with your own food while you are having your meal or to give it a biscuit while you are drinking tea or coffee. By doing this, you encourage begging-behaviour and that of course stimulates slavering.
During socialisation you have to be aware of the fact that it is very important for your Bullmastiff to meet enough different people, children and other animals. The Bullmastiff is very gentle with children, but a clumsy puppy can knock down a small child accidentally. This certainly is not done on purpose, because the Bullmastiff really can take a lot from children. The Bullmastiff also is a very tolerant dog towards other pets.

Male or female?

Whether you buy a male or a female is mainly a question of personal preference. Both can grow up to become attractive and well behaved members of the family. And as far as working capacity is concerned, there is no difference between a dog and a bitch. Males sometimes seem somewhat more self-assured and can display dominant

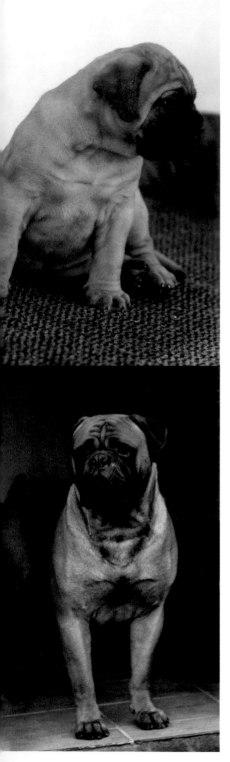

behaviour, trying to play boss over other dogs, especially over other males, and, if they get the chance, over humans too. In the wild the most dominant dog (or wolf) is always the leader of the pack. In many cases this is a male.

It is of the utmost importance for a good relationship between dog and master that the dog understands from the outset that you are the leader of the pack. This demands an understanding yet consistent upbringing.

When females become fertile, usually between eight and twelve months, they go on heat. This happens twice per year and lasts two to three weeks. This is the fertile period when a female can mate and, especially during the second half of their season, they will try to go out in search of a male. Measures need to be taken to prevent unwanted additions to the family. A male will display more masculine behaviour once he becomes sexually mature. He will make clear to other dogs which territory is his by urinating frequently and in as many places as possible. He's also difficult to confine when there is a bitch in season in the area. However, as far as general care is concerned, there is little difference between male and female.

A puppy test is good for defining what kind of character a young dog will develop. During this test one usually sees that a dog is more dominant than a bitch. You can often quickly recognise the bossy, the adventurous and the cautious characters. So visit the litter a couple of times early on. Try to pick a puppy that suits your own personality. A dominant dog, for instance, needs a strong hand. It will often try to see how far it can go. You must regularly make it clear who's the boss, and that it must obey all the members of the family.

Puppy or adult dog?

After you have made the decision for a male or female, the next question comes up. Should it be a puppy or an adult dog? Your household circumstances usually play a major role here.

Of course, it is great having a sweet little puppy in the house, but bringing up a young dog requires a lot of time. In the first year of its life it learns more than during the rest of its life. This is the period when the foundations are laid for elementary matters such as house-training, obedience and social behaviour. You should reckon on, especially in the first few months, having to devote a lot of time to caring for your puppy and bringing it up. You would not need so much time with a grown dog. It has already been brought up, but this does not mean it will not need correcting from time to time.

A puppy will no doubt leave a trail of destruction in its wake for the first few months. With a little bad luck, this will cost you a number of rolls of wallpaper, some good shoes and a few socks. In the worst case you'll be left with some chewed furniture. Some puppies even manage to tear curtains from their rails. With good upbringing this 'vandalism' will quickly disappear, but you will not have to worry about this if you get an older dog.

The greatest advantage of a puppy, of course, is that you can bring it up your own way. The upbringing a dog gets or does not get is a major influence on its whole character. Finally, financial aspects may play a role in your choice.
A puppy is generally much more expensive than an adult dog, not only in purchase price but also in maintenance. A puppy needs to go to the veterinarian more often for the necessary vaccinations and check-ups. Overall, bringing up a puppy requires a good deal of energy, time and money, but you have its upbringing in your own hands. An adult dog requires less money and time, but its character is already formed. You should also try to find out about the background of an adult dog. Its previous owner may have formed its character in somewhat less positive ways.

Two dogs?

Having two or more dogs in the house is not just nice for us, but also for the animals themselves. Dogs get a lot of pleasure from each others' company. After all, they are pack animals. Bear in mind that a Bullmastiff is a rather big dog. Try to estimate very well, if you have the suitable house to be able to give your two Bullmastiffs a good home. If you are sure that you want two young dogs, it is best not to buy them at the same time. Bringing a dog up and establishing the bond between dog and master takes time and you need to give a lot of attention to the dog in this phase. Having two puppies in the house means you have to divide your attention. Apart from that, there is a chance that they will focus on one another rather than on their master.

Buy the second pup when the first is (almost) an adult. Two adult dogs can happily be brought into the household together. Taking in a puppy when the first dog is somewhat older often has a positive effect on the older dog. The influence of the puppy seems almost to give it a second childhood. The older dog, if it has been well brought up, can help with the upbringing of the puppy. Young dogs like to imitate the behaviour of their elders. Do not forget to give both dogs the same amount of attention. Take the puppy out alone at least once per day during the first eighteen months. Ensure both dogs get enough peace and quiet. You have to force Bullmastiffs to do this by separating them after a romp, because they never want to stop.

It is inadvisable to keep two male Bullmastiffs together. Male Bullmastiffs are too dominant to live together. For the first eighteen months they will pretend that everything is fine. But just when you lean back satisfied, because you think that you have succeeded after all, they attack each other and can no longer be kept in the same room.

The combination of a male and female needs special attention. If you do not plan to breed with your dogs, you must take measures to prevent them mating when the bitch is in season. Spaying the bitch or neutering the male are possibilities, but the latter is usually only done on medical advice, or for behavioural reasons.

The Bullmastiff and children

Dogs and children are a great combination. They can play together and get great pleasure from each other. Moreover, children need to learn how to handle living beings; they develop respect and a sense of responsibility by caring for a dog, or other pets. However sweet a dog is, children must understand that a dog is a living being and not a toy. A dog is not comfortable when it is being messed around with. It can become frightened, timid and even aggressive. So make it clear what a dog likes and what it does not. Look for ways the child can play with the dog, perhaps a game of hide-and-seek, where the child hides and the dog has to find it. Even a simple tennis ball can give enormous pleasure. Children must learn to leave a dog in peace when it does not want to play anymore. The dog must also have its own place where it is not disturbed. Have children help with your dog's care as much as possible. A strong bond will be the result.

You must bear in mind that some Bullmastiffs are fanatical game players and may sometimes snap at a hand, just as at a ball or another toy. They can also jump high and hard in their over-enthusiasm, and you must then really try to calm the dog down.

A young Bullmastiff with its limitless energy often will not know when to stop, and you must usually pick the moment when the game is over. A cage or an indoor kennel can be useful here, because a dog needs regular periods of rest for its growth.

The arrival of a baby also means changes in the life of a dog. Before the birth you can help get the dog acquainted with the new situation. Let it sniff at the new things in the house and it will quickly accept them. When the baby has arrived involve the dog as much as possible in day-by-day events, but make sure it gets plenty of attention too. NEVER leave a dog alone with young children. Crawling infants sometimes make unexpected movements, which can easily frighten a dog. Infants are hugely curious, and may try to find out whether the tail is really fastened to the dog, or whether it can get its eyes out, just like it can with its cuddly toys. A dog is a dog and it will defend itself when it feels threatened.

Sometimes children want to take the dog out for a walk. For the child this might be a sign of being independent. Even if your Bullmastiff is very obedient, the child lacks the power and authority over the dog. Whenever it gets irritated by another dog on the street, or gets sight of something else, a child can NEVER correct a Bullmastiff. NEVER, NEVER allow a child to go for a walk with your Bullmastiff.

A dog and cats

Despite the fact that their body language is very different, dogs and cats can actually get on a lot better with each other than many people think.

For example, a dog lying on its back is submissive. A cat lying on its back is not at all submissive, but makes sure that it has its best weapons of defence, i.e. its claws, at its disposal. However, dogs and cats have one thing in common: they growl when they are angry, and both animals understand this.

As far as nutrients are concerned, dogs and cats must not share each other's food. Dog food may lack high enough levels of taurine, which is essential for cats. Dogs and cats must also not share a food bowl, as a dog will not tolerate another animal sharing its bowl. A persistent kitten might therefore get a serious ticking off from your dog. Playing together is fine, but you must prevent your pets eating together.

Some dogs will love to chase your cat around. You must prohibit this behaviour from the very beginning. The cat also has its rights and the dog will have to learn not to chase everything that moves. You can take your dog to special classes to help deal with this. Some dogs (this is not a characteristic of any particular breed) love to eat cat faeces (coprophagia). To prevent your dog eating from the cat litter, place the litter box in another room, where only your cat has access. Or place the litter box between two pieces of furniture in a manner that prevents your dog gaining access.

Where to buy your dog

There are various ways of acquiring a dog. The decision for a puppy or an adult dog will also define for the most part where to buy your dog.

If it has to be a puppy, then you need to find a breeder with a litter. If you chose a popular breed, like the Bullmastiff, there is enough choice. But you may also face the problem that there are so many puppies on sale that have only been bred for profit's sake. You can see how many puppies are for sale by looking in the regional newspaper every Saturday. Some of these dogs have a pedigree, but many do not.

These breeders very often do not watch out for breed-specific illnesses, nor for inbreeding or any hereditary breeding faults and defects; puppies are separated from their mother as fast as possible and are thus insufficiently socialised. NEVER buy a puppy that is too young, or whose mother you were not able to see. Always buy a puppy through the breed association.

Fortunately there are also enough bona-fide breeders of Bullmastiffs who have been involved with the breed for many years as serious breeders and exhibitors and they are only too willing to help you get your Bullmastiff. Try to visit a number of breeders before you actually buy your puppy. Check the parent dogs' papers to ensure they were free of Hip Dysplasia (HD) and of hereditary eye diseases. Ask if the breeder is prepared to help you after you have bought your puppy, and to help you find solutions for any problems that may come up.

We recommend you buy a Bullmastiff through the breed clubs. Breeders who are members of the association must fulfil its breeding rules. Any breeder that does not stick to these strict conditions is expelled. Under these rules the parents must be examined for hip dysplasia and must be heart tested with a grade not higher than 1.

The puppy services of the breed clubs can help you with addresses for reliable breeders. The breed federation exercises a very strict breeding policy intended to keep the Bullmastiff population healthy and free of congenital defects. It also allows its members to breed only with animals that are registered with The Kennel Club or with foreign clubs recognised by The Kennel Club.

The breed clubs may be able to inform you about available puppies of breeders who are members of the association. They will often publish lists of litters that have been bred according to their guidelines. To be recognised as a breeder by the breed associations, a breeder must fulfil certain requirements, such as having the parent's heart tested with grades not higher than 1.
Some breed associations also have a puppy information service, where you can get information about puppies available within the association. They also help to place adult dogs that can no longer be kept by their owners due to personal circumstances (divorce, moving home etc.).

Finally, you must also realise that a pedigree is nothing more or less than evidence of descent. The Kennel Club also awards pedigree certificates to the offspring of parents that suffer from hereditary defects, or that have not been examined for these. A pedigree says nothing about the health of the parents.

Things to watch out for

Buying a puppy is no simple matter. You must pay attention to the following:
- Never buy a puppy on an impulse, even if it is love at first sight. A dog is a living being that will need a lot of care and attention over a long period. It is not a toy that you can put away when you are done with it. You choose a dog to be a comrade and companion for many years.
- Take a good look at the mother. Is she calm, nervous, aggressive, well cared-for or neglected? The behaviour and condition of the mother is not only a sign of the quality of the breeder, but also of the puppy you are about to buy.
- Avoid buying a puppy whose mother was kept only in a kennel. A young dog needs as many stimuli and experiences as possible during its early months, including family life. It can thus get used to humans, other pets and different sights and sounds. Kennel dogs miss these experiences and have not been sufficiently socialised.
- Always ask to see the papers of the parents (vaccination certificates, pedigrees, official reports on health examinations such as hip- and eye-checks).
- Ask whether the pups have been vaccinated and wormed or not. Puppies must be vaccinated in the 6th, 9th and between the 12th and 14th week. Regular worming is also extremely important. The first worming has to be done when the puppies are 3 weeks old and after that every two weeks.
- Never buy a puppy younger than eight weeks.
- Put any agreement with the breeder in writing. A model agreement is available from the Kennel Club or from the Breed Association.

Shopping list
- Collar
- Lead
- ID tag
- Blanket
- Water bowl
- Food bowl
- Poop scoop
- Dry food
- Canned food
- Comb
- Brush
- Toys
- Dog basket
- Indoor kennel

Ten golden puppy rules

1. Walk your puppy in doses followed by one hour play, a feed and then three hours sleep.
2. Never let a puppy run endlessly after a ball or a stick.
3. Do not let your puppy romp wildly with large, heavy dogs.
4. Do not let your puppy play on a full stomach.
5. Do not give your puppy anything to drink straight after its food.
6. Do not let your puppy go up and down the stairs in its first year. Also be careful with smooth floors.
7. Never add supplements to ready-made dogfood.
8. Watch you puppy's weight. Being overweight can lead to bone abnormalities.
9. Give your puppy a quiet place to sleep.
10. Pick up your puppy carefully, one hand under its chest and the other hand under its hindquarters.

Travelling

Travelling with a dog is not always pure pleasure. Some dogs love a ride in the car while others need huge efforts to even get them in it. Some dogs suffer from car-sickness their whole life. If you are planning a holiday in far-away places and want to take your dog with you, you should ask yourself whether you are really doing it a favour.

Travelling with your Bullmastiff
NEVER, NEVER leave your Bullmastiff unattended in a car, not even for a few minutes. Never travel long distances with your Bullmastiff in the car, unless you make adequate provision in case of an emergency. Even if you have air conditioning in your car, you should not take your Bullmastiff with you on long distances. Take plenty of cool water with you and make sure that it has suitable shade from the sun. There also has to be a free flow of air through the car. During very hot weather you can use semi frozen bottles of water (the square plastic bottles are ideal). When they thaw they will give you a supply of ice cold water. Placed in the box of your Bullmastiff and covered with a towel, this will also help to keep your dog cool. If you put wet towels in the freezer and then store them in a cool box they make an excellent cool bed for your dog to lie on. The lightweight canvas cages are not recommended to use for your Bullmastiff, as they do not allow an adequate airflow.
Before you plan to travel to a show, think about all this. Remember that there is no prize or championship at a dog show, which is ever worth the life of your Bullmastiff.
STRESS AND HEAT ARE A LETHAL COMBINATION.

That very first trip
The first trip of a puppy's life is also the most nerve-wrecking. This is the trip from the breeder's to its new home. If possible, pick up your puppy in the early morning. Then it will have the whole day to get used to the new environment.

Ask the breeder not to feed your puppy on that day. The young animal will be overwhelmed by all kinds of new experiences. First of all, it goes away from its mother and its littermates; it has to go into a small room (the car) with all its new smells, noises and strange people. So there is a big chance that the puppy will be car-sick this first time, with the annoying consequence that it will remember travelling in the car as an unpleasant experience.

So it is important to make this first trip as pleasant as possible. When picking up a puppy, always take someone with you who can sit on the back seat with the puppy on his or her lap and talk to it calmly. If it is too warm in the car for the puppy, a place on the floor at the feet of your companion is ideal. The pup will lie there relatively quietly and may even take a nap. Ask the breeder for a cloth or something else from the puppies' basket or bed that carries a familiar scent. The puppy can lie on this in the car, and this will also help if it feels lonely during the first nights at home. If the trip home is a long one, then stop for a break once in a while. Let your puppy roam and sniff around on the lead, offer it a little bit to drink and, if necessary, let it do its business. And take care to lay an old towel in the car. It can happen that the puppy, in its nervousness, may urinate or be sick. It is also good advice to give a puppy positive experiences with car journeys. Make short trips to nice places where you can walk and play with it. After all, once in a while you will have to take your dog to certain places, such as to the veterinarian or to visit friends or acquaintances.

Taking your Bullmastiff on holiday

When making holiday plans, you also need to think about what you are going to do with your dog during that time. Are you taking it with you, putting it into a boarding kennel or leaving it with friends? In any event there are a number of things you need to do in good time. If you want to take your dog with you, you need to be sure before you leave that your dog will be welcome at your holiday home, and you also need to check what rules there are. If you are going abroad it will need certain vaccinations and a health certificate, which normally needs to be done four weeks before departure. You must also be sure that you have made all the arrangements necessary to bring your dog back home to the UK, without it needing to go into quarantine under the rabies regulations. Your vet can give you the most recent information.

If your trip goes to southern Europe, ask for a treatment against ticks (you can read more about this in the chapter on parasites).

Although dog-owners usually enjoy taking their dog on holiday, you must seriously ask yourself if the dog is going to enjoy it as well. Bullmastiffs certainly do not feel comfortable in a hot country.

Days spent on travelling in a car are equally unpleasant for many dogs, and as we already saw, some dogs suffer badly from car-sickness. There are good medicines to prevent this, but they can also have side-effects and it is questionable if you are doing your dog a favour with these medicines. In case you do decide to take your dog with you, make regular stops at safe places during your journey, so that your dog can have a good run. Take plenty of fresh drinking water with you, as well as the food your dog is used to. Never leave your dog in the car when the sun is shining. The temperature can climb fast and this can very quickly become an awful and life-threatening situation for your dog. If you cannot avoid it, park the car in the shade as far as possible and leave a window open for a little fresh air. Even if you have taken these precautions, frequently check on your dog and never stay away longer than is strictly necessary.

If you are travelling by plane or ship, make sure in good time that your dog can travel with you and what rules you need to observe. You will need some time to make all the arrangements. Maybe you decide not to take your dog with you, and then you must find a place where your dog can stay. There are special boarding kennels for Bullmastiffs. Arrangements for a place in a boarding kennel need to be made well in advance, and there may be certain vaccinations required, which need to be given at least one month before the stay.

If your dog cannot be accommodated in the homes of relatives or friends, it might be possible to have an acquaintance stay in your house. This also needs to be arranged well in advance, as it might be difficult to find someone who can look after your dog. Always ensure that your dog can be traced in case it should run away or get lost while you are on holiday. A little tube with your address or a tag with home and holiday address and a mobile telephone number can prevent a lot of problems.

Moving home

Dogs generally become more attached to humans than to the house they live in. Moving home is usually not a problem for them. But it can be useful before moving to let the dog get to know its new home and the area around it.

If you can, leave your dog with relatives or friends or in a boarding kennel on the day of the move. The chance of it running away or getting lost is then practically zero. When your move is complete, you can pick your dog up and let it quietly get familiar with its new home and environment. Give it its own place in the house at once and it will quickly adapt.

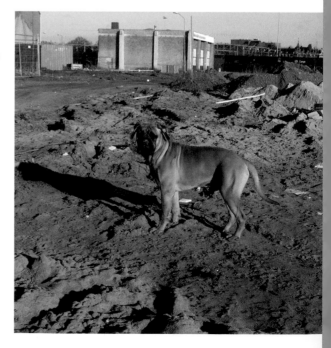

During the first week or so, always walk your dog on a lead, because an animal can also get lost in new surroundings. Always take a different route so it quickly gets to know the neighbourhood.

Do not forget to get your new address and phone number engraved on the dog's tag. Send a change of address notice to the institution that has the microchip or tattoo data (in the UK tattooing is not very common). In some communities dogs need to be registered.

Keep Your Bullmastiff Cool
A heat stroke can kill your Bullmastiff
Heat stroke is an emergency, which can be life threatening. For that reason it is important that Bullmastiff owners learn to recognise the signs of a heat stroke. The dog will require immediate treatment. Bullmastiffs do not tolerate high temperatures as well as we humans do. Most short faced breeds have these problems. Dogs cannot sweat, they can only depend on rapid breathing to keep cool. By exchanging warm air when they breathe out with cooler surrounding air as they breathe in, they manage to regulate their body temperature. It is obvious, that when the air temperature is close to body temperature, cooling by rapid breathing will not be very succeful.

Signs of a heat stroke
A heat stroke is evident by the typical appearance of the dog, and it can be confirmed by taking its temperature. A heat stroke starts with rapid, frantic, noisy, breathing.The tongue and the inside of the mouth are bright red. The dog's saliva is thick and hangs in drools or it may appear frothy. The dog frequently vomits. The eyes have a frantic bulbous look. Your Bullmastiff really will be in serious trouble if these signs continue, as within a very short time the dog's lips and tongue turn blue and the eyes may glaze over. The dog becomes unsteady and staggers. It may have diarrhoea and it will become progressively weaker. Coma and death can follow. All this happens within a few minutes.

Treatment
When you think that your dog is overheating, you have to take emergency measures immediately. When it is not too bad, you can move the dog to cooler surroundings and frequently offer it a small amount of water.
In case the dog is showing more serious signs (as described above) or if you are not sure about it, you can cool down your Bullmastiff by immersion of its body in cool water, or by being hosed down with a garden hose. In emergency cases an ice cube gently inserted in the rectum also helps. A heat stroke can also be accompanied by swelling of the throat, the dog will 'roar' or 'rasp' when breathing, which aggravates the problem by reducing the airflow, causing the dog to panic and get even more stressed. This situation requires veterinary treatment immediately, the vet will usually administer a cortisone injection to reduce swelling. He may also administer a cool water enema.

Prevention
Do not expose your Bullmastiff to prolonged heat. Restrict exercise during the heat of the day. Provide your Bullmastiff with shade and water if you are outside, even in the garden. See that your Bullmastiff does not get overexcited or stressed during hot weather.

Feeding

A dog will actually eat a lot more than just meat. In the wild it would eat its prey complete with skin and fur, including the bones, stomach and intestines with their semi-digested vegetable material. In this way the dog supplements its meat menu with the vitamins and minerals it needs. This is also the basis for feeding a domestic dog.

Basic principles of dog food
In general
Dogs have always been primarily carnivores (meat eaters). A minor part of their daily diet consists of vegetable material or the vegetable-based content of their prey's stomach and intestines. In the past, dogs kept as pets used to be fed the remains of the family dinner.

Nowadays, most dogs are fed a diet of dry food and/or canned food. The diets of our domestic dogs and cats have changed remarkably over the last fifteen years. There has been a clear increase in expertise and the foodstuffs have become increasingly differentiated. To fully understand the effects of foods, it is important to have some understanding of the anatomy and physiology of dogs.

Anatomy and physiology of the dog's digestive tract
Ingested food first passes into the mouth, where it is crunched. Dogs have no lateral movement in their jaws and therefore cannot chew, but during this crunching, the food is divided into smaller bits and moistened with saliva.

The dog's saliva does not include digestive enzymes, so true digestion does not yet start in the mouth. After swallowing, the food passes through the oesophagus to the stomach, where it is mixed and kneaded with gastric acid, i.e. one of the digestive juices. The gastric acid breaks down the proteins present in the food and kills off a large number of potentially harmful micro-organisms present in the food.

Once the food pulp has been kneaded through thoroughly and fulfils a number of chemical requirements, the closing muscle (pylorus) of the stomach relaxes and the food passes through into the duodenum.
The duodenum is the first part of the small intestine. Here important digestive juices such as gall and the pancreatic juices are added to the food pulp. The gall juices help with the digestion of fat and the pancreatic juices contain enzymes which help with the digestion of carbohydrates, proteins and fat.
Enzymes are substances which are produced by the animal itself and which help with chemical transformation during digestion.
The small intestine must furthermore be differentiated into the jejunum, ileum and caecum (appendix). The wall of the small intestine contains cells which provide the digestive juices. The wall has plenty of folds to provide as large a surface area as possible, where bacteria, which help in the digestive processes, and enzymes find a place to attach to. The actual digestion occurs in the small intestine and the foodstuffs are cut down into tiny pieces which can be absorbed.

After being absorbed by the cells in the intestines, the nutrients are passed on to the blood, which transports the nutrients to the liver. The liver functions as a sort of traffic agent, which decides what needs to happen to the different nutrients and then sends them to the right place.

The large intestine (colon) follows on from the small intestine. The most important function here is to absorb the water from the food pulp. The intestine ends in the closing muscle (anus) via the rectum.

Food
Food contains many nutrients which can be divided into six important groups: proteins, fats, carbohydrates, minerals, vitamins and water. Life cannot exist without water. Water does not actually contain any extra nutrients, unless it is mineral water, which can be very rich in certain minerals.

Proteins
Proteins look like a pearl necklace, consisting of different amino acids (the pearls). The amount and type of amino acids determines the characteristics of the protein in question.
The presence of nitrogen in all amino acids is important for the development of tissue.

Proteins fulfil many functions in the body; they are the most important components of tissue, hormones and enzymes. Furthermore, they fulfil other important roles by maintaining water levels in the body, removing toxins and maintaining a good defence system.

Proteins are found in both vegetable (grains, legumes, yeast) and animal (meat, fish, poultry, eggs) form. An adult dog must have at least (20g protein/1000kcal food) 8% protein in the dry matter of its food (NRC 1985; NRC 2006) to keep up the maintenance level. In fact, if you want to ensure optimum health, maximum performance and a beautiful appearance, this percentage must be somewhat higher.

The story that protein is bad for dogs has long been proven a myth. This was based on research in rats, but at the end of the 70s, research showed that the kidney metabolism of dogs is by no means as sensitive as that of rats. Since 1993, we have also known that proteins do not have a detrimental influence on growth.

On the contrary, proteins, together with the right exercise, contribute to healthy muscles, which in turn stabilise the skeleton. This is a very important consideration for such conditions as hip dysplasia, for example.
Plenty of proteins therefore contribute to your dog's health.

A shortage of proteins will lead to anaemia, low resistance to illness, loss of muscle tissue, etc. A shortage of proteins is caused not only by insufficient absorption, but also through increased breaking-down of proteins, which may be caused by many forms of stress (mental or physical strain on the individual animal).
An influence of protein on behaviour is not yet clear.

Fat
The most important function of fats is to provide energy. Besides this, fats also provide unsaturated fatty acids. Fatty acids fulfil important functions in the nervous systems and the skin's metabolism, among other things. Fats in the food are very easily digested by dogs; in general they digest as much as 95 - 98%.

Dogs, just as humans, prefer food with a higher fat content, which is why it is often added to dog food to make it 'tastier'. Fat is also important as it stores some vitamins.

Carbohydrates

Carbohydrates always originate in vegetable material.

Starch and sugar are well-known examples of carbohydrates.

You can differentiate between digestible carbohydrates (starch, simple sugars) and non-digestible carbohydrates (cellulose, pectin), which come from the cell membranes and fibres of plants.

Carbohydrates improve the transport of the food pulp in the intestines by stimulating the membrane of the intestines. This stimulates the peristaltic movement of the intestines.

A disadvantage is that they increase the volume of the faeces, as they also hold a lot of water. A good compromise are the fibres which function as such throughout the major part of the intestines, and are then broken down at the last stage by bacteria in the large intestine. The fibres are broken down into substances which partly function as a source of food for the cells of the large intestine. Beet pulp, for example, contains these valuable fibres.

Minerals

Minerals only play a minor role in your dog's diet as far as the amount is concerned, but they are absolutely vital. Because minerals are needed in such small amounts, mistakes are easily made.

Minerals are divided into macro-minerals and micro-minerals or trace elements. Calcium (Ca) and phosphorus (P) are well-known macro-minerals. They fulfil an important role in building up the skeleton and, depending on the physiological phase, must be provided by the food in a fixed relation to each other. As phosphorus is of vegetable origin, it can often not be absorbed from the food, as in this form phosphorus cannot be absorbed by dogs (phytate).

Other important macro-elements include: magnesium (Mg) (skeleton, enzymes), sodium (Na), potassium (K) and chlorine (Cl). Some examples of micro-minerals include: iron (Fe) (blood, oxygen transport), copper (Cu) (creation of pigment, blood), zinc (Zn) (enzymes, skin), manganese (Mn) (enzymes), iodine (I) (thyroid hormone) and selenium (Se) (muscle tissue, anti-oxidant).

Vitamins

Vitamins can be of both vegetable and animal origins. Vitamins are divided into water-soluble and non-water-soluble vitamins. Vitamins are also required only in very small amounts and dogs can produce a number of vitamins themselves. Below, we will list a number of important vitamins and their functions.

Some important functions of vitamins

	function	shortage	excess
vitamin A	fertility, skin and eyes	fertility problems, night blindness	abnormal bone metabolism vitamin K deficiency
vitamin D3	bone metabolism	abnormal bone metabolism	abnormal bone metabolism, kidney malfunction
vitamin E	with Se protection, muscle cells, anti-oxidant	fertility problems, muscle dystrophy	
vitamin K	blood clotting	haemorrhages	
vitamin C	collagen metabolism, resistance, mucous membranes	connective tissue damage, haemorrhages, liver necrosis	
B1 (thimaine)	carbohydrate metabolism, nervous system	anorexia, circulation problems, diarrhoea, atrophic reproductive organs	
B2 (riboflavine)	catalyst, energy production, protein metabolism	anorexia, growth delays, circulation problems	
PP (niacine)	catalyst, resistance, skin and mucous membranes	skin problems, anorexia, diarrhoea	
B3 (pantothene acid)	part of coenzyme A, Krebs-cycle	alopecia, anorexia, diarrhoea	
B6 (pyridoxine)	catalyst protein metabolism	skin problems, haematological problems	
biotine	catalyst fatty acid synthesis	coat and skin problems	
folic acid	catalyst AZ synthesis	haematological and skin problems	
B12 (cyanocobalamine)	catalyst cystine/ methiomine metabolism	anaemia, alopecia, growth problems	

Energy

All organic processes require energy. This energy is needed for the body to function, produce tissue and to maintain body temperature, for example. The energy required must be provided by food. In principal, dogs eat until they have fulfilled their energy requirements. However, due to causes such as boredom, the feeding regime and tastiness of the food, there are many dogs that eat more than they need and become fat and heavy. It is therefore important to regularly check your dog's condition.

A dog will store energy reserves as fat on the ribcage. On short-haired dogs, you must be able to see the last two ribs, and on long-haired dogs you must be able to feel the ribs.

Start feeding your dog with the amount recommended on the food packaging, check your dog's condition once per week and adapt it as necessary. Increase the amount of food if you feel the ribs too clearly, and decrease the amount if you can no longer feel the ribs easily. Particularly puppies of breeds prone to skeletal growth problems must be somewhat on the thinner side while growing up.

Industrial food

Industrial dog foods can be divided into three categories depending on their moisture content: moist, semi-moist and dry food. Moist foods contain 70 - 85% water. Their high moisture content makes them very tasty for dogs, but they spoil more easily. The quality is more difficult to maintain than with dry food. The transport is also a disadvantage for the environment and for the owner: four times as much volume needs to be transported. This type of food is also relatively expensive.

Semi-moist food is dry enough that it does not have to be packed into cans. There are no real advantages to this type of food. Dogs might accept it somewhat more easily than dry food, but it does spoil quite easily due to its higher moisture content. Due to their increased moisture content, frozen foods may also be added to this category.

Dry foods are the most economical and are also not prone to turning mouldy, which means that they keep for a comparatively long time. The specific manufacturing process makes it easier to ensure constant high quality levels. Technically speaking, mixers belong to dry food until they have had water added. At this point, they also spoil quite quickly.
If you want to compare different types of food with each other, you will need to look at the dry matter (= product without water) contents and ingredients.

It is very difficult to judge the quality of dog food. The packaging does not provide all the information and may also not contain any quality claims. It is therefore a matter of trust and you might want to request some further information from the manufacturer. The amount of faeces also gives an indication: the more faeces, the lower the food quality. This, however, does not apply to fibre-rich foods, such as diet foods, "light foods", senior foods and diabetic foods.

Food quality
There are a number of important points as regards the quality of dog food: the digestibility, the biological value (degree to which the nutrients can be absorbed into the tissue), the manufacturing process and the circumstances under which the food is kept until consumption.
Different terminology is used to indicate quality levels. At the moment, the product range includes super premium, premium, products for the medium segment and products for the economical segment. The lower the quality, the lower the price per kilogram. Top quality can only be delivered by manufacturers who have the best raw materials available, who conduct thorough research and who have a technologically advanced manufacturing process.
The first threat to the quality is oxidization of the ingredients. Light, oxygen and warmth are threats to food quality. Anti-oxidants therefore do a good job and the user must also ensure hygienic handling of the food. Good-quality food is packaged in an airtight packaging, which also keeps out the light, it has a batch code and can tell you the best before and the manufacture dates.

Physiological phases

Good feeding must be adapted as well as possible to the physiological phase of the individual dog. After all, the physiological phase it is in determines what a dog needs. A growing dog must produce a lot more tissue and therefore needs more building blocks than an adult dog.

All these growth processes require a lot of energy, which means that the energy need is also higher. Depending on the size of the dog, it will grow for 7 to 18 or even 24 months. During the growing period the puppy's digestive system is not fully developed and so can only cope with small volumes of food.

It is therefore important that the food is both energy dense (which allows for a smaller feeding volume) and balanced in nutrients for that age and stage in development.

Puppies from a number of usually larger breeds have an increased risk of bone-related growth problems and must therefore be fed specifically adapted food. It is also important to keep these puppies slim when they are growing.

Reproduction and lactation are highly demanding on the bitch and, considering that she has to produce both offspring and milk, you can imagine that her energy needs increase a lot. From the 6th week of the pregnancy, you will therefore need to adapt the amount you food. Energy demands also increase if your dog is very active. If there is a lot of stress on muscle tissue, it will need to be repaired from time to time. There is also increasing 'wear' on the blood, which means that more nutrients are needed to produce plenty of blood cells. If you keep your dog in an outdoor kennel, it might also require more energy, as it will lose warmth more easily and it might be more active due to being kept outdoors.

By having a close look at the needs of dogs in different physiological phases, it is possible to develop a food which fulfils specific requirements under certain circumstances. Obviously, such dog food requires a lot more research and high-quality raw materials, which will be reflected in a somewhat higher price. An adequate dog food will ensure optimum health and resistance and is therefore always worth the asking price.

Besides the physiological phase, the size of the dog also matters. Pedigree dogs, of course, have set size standards and on mongrels the size depends on the parent animals. Research has shown that there are many differences between small and large dogs; both in terms of susceptibility to health problems and in anatomy and physiology. The manufacturers of the best dog foods take these differences into account. To give just a few examples of the physiological differences between large and small dog breeds:

	Small dog	Difference*	Large dog
Growth period	8 months	3	24 months
Range of growth	20x birth weight	5	100x birth weight
Length canine tooth	4-5 mm	3	15-16 mm
Energy needs	132 Kcal/kg BW**	3	45 Kcal/kg BW**
Weight digestive tract	7% BW**	>2	2.8% BW**
Life expectancy	> 12 years	+/- 3	7 years

* Difference = factor ** BW = body weight

Of course, breeds have their specific size requirements, and every breed also has its own characteristics, such as a special coat or even breed-specific conditions. Breed-specific foods are therefore becoming increasingly popular. These foods are based on the special nutritional needs of the breed and some foods also contain substances which help to prevent breed-specific conditions developing.

Over the last few years, increasing attention has been paid to the possible effect of dog food in addressing potential health risks. Certain substances are added to the food, for example to increase the burning of fat (L-carnitine), to prevent diarrhoea in puppies (zeolite), to support the cartilage (glucosamine and chondroitin sulphate), etc. The right food can therefore make a major contribution to your dog's health.

Important guidelines

In general
Buy food only in an undamaged package and have experts (vet, pet shop owner or breeder) advise you. Buying in bulk might be economical, but make sure that you have a food bin. Put a week's supply in a bucket, for example, and place the rest in a food bin in a dark, cool, place. Always make sure that you use up or throw away the last bit and clean out the bin regularly!

Puppy food
Buy the most suitable food for your puppy. The basis for a healthy adult life is laid in the growth period and food plays an important role here.

Adult dog
Choose the food which best suits your dog and adapt the amount you feed to its condition.

Pregnant dog
The food requirements of the bitch increase from the 6th week of pregnancy. In the past, bitches were often fed puppy food in the last stage of the pregnancy or during lactation. However, with today's range of puppy foods, they might not all be suitable, so get expert advice on how best to feed your pregnant bitch.

Older dog
The food requirements of older dogs change quite a lot. Scientifically speaking, older dogs need more easily digestible food, which stimulates the intestines, a normal protein content with high biological value and some support for the heart, the skeleton and to improve resistance to illness.

Puppies, pregnant bitch and mother

Amount of food during pregnancy and suckling period

To ensure that the weight increase is no more than 20% on large bitches and no more than 30% on small bitches, it is important to keep a close eye on the weight of your pregnant bitch.

The more the weight increases, the higher the risk of problems during the birth. During pregnancy and suckling, the bitch must be fed a correctly composed diet to ensure that her food reserves are not completely exhausted. If she is fed an incorrect diet, the bitch will have far more trouble recovering from this very demanding period.

During pregnancy

A bitch is pregnant for approximately 63 days. Her food needs start to increase at around the 5th or 6th week of pregnancy. About 25% of the foetus develops during the first 6 weeks of the pregnancy; the remaining 75% of the foetus develops from weeks 6 to 9.

During the last trimester, your bitch will have a particularly high need for:

Energy: + 50 to 70%
Proteins: + 170 to 180%
Minerals: ++ (calcium, phosphorus)
Vitamins: ++

During suckling

The suckling period lasts for 4 to 5 weeks, and the puppies gradually suckle less from the 4th week on. While suckling her offspring, the bitch will have a much higher energy need, as she must also produce the food for them. The mother's milk is very rich in energy and proteins. It is therefore important that the bitch is fed a diet which is high in energy and proteins, and which is very easily digestible. The actual food requirements vary a lot and primarily depend on the size of the litter. The food needs of a suckling bitch may be as follows:

Energy: + 325%
Proteins: + 725%
Minerals: ++++ (calcium, phosphorus)
Vitamins: ++++

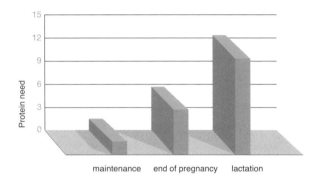

To prevent digestive problems, it is advisable to feed the bitch the same food from the last part of the pregnancy until the time that the puppies are fully weaned. The bitch's intestines are particularly sensitive to food changes during this important period. Within 24 hours, a puppy suckles more than twenty times from its mother. The bitch must produce 20 to 25% of a puppy's weight in milk to feed one puppy for one day (so multiply this by the number of puppies in the litter).

The bitch may be fed ad lib during the suckling period, but do keep an eye on her condition.

Colostrum is the first milk that the bitch produces after the puppies are born. It is therefore very important that the puppies drink their mother's milk within the first 24 hours after birth. The colostrum contains anti-bodies against infections, which gives the puppies a good start to build up their own solid resistance. If the bitch produces too little milk, you will need to supplement it with special puppy milk.

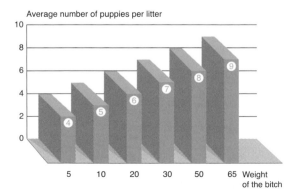

Puppy during weaning

Right after being born, the puppies depend entirely on their mother's milk as their only food source to stay alive.

It is very important to check your puppies' growth during the first few days by weighing them at exactly the same time every day. Weaning must go very smoothly, so that the puppy and its organs get used to a completely new diet. When the puppy must change from a liquid diet to a solid diet, it is advisable to do this via an extra step.

Energy: + 50 to 70%
Proteins: + 170 to 180%
Minerals: ++ (calcium, phosphorus)
Vitamins: ++

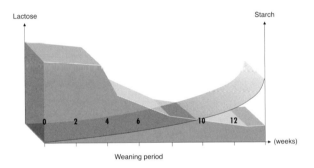

Weaning period

The increasing nutritional needs are best fulfilled by feeding the bitch a specifically composed diet from the fifth or sixth week on. Besides more energy, the bitch also needs more proteins and she needs a concentrated and easily digestible diet, as the uterus pushes onto the stomach during pregnancy, which decreases the stomach volume. The bitch therefore can no longer deal with large amounts of food.

Weaning - an important period

The first step in weaning begins after the third week, when you can start feeding the puppies small amounts of moistened food. During the weaning period, the puppies are quite prone to diarrhoea, which is at least partly due to their limited ability to digest starch. Compared to an adult dog, they only have a 5 - 10% ability to digest starch (see picture). To minimise the risk of diarrhoea and to ensure optimum digestion, feed the puppy a food which is easily digestible and which has a low starch content.

Ready-made foods

It is not easy for a layman to put together a complete menu for a dog, which includes all the necessary proteins, fats, vitamins and minerals in just the right proportions and quantities. Meat alone is certainly not a complete meal for a dog. It contains too little calcium. A calcium deficiency over time will lead to bone defects, and for a fast-growing puppy this can lead to serious skeletal deformities.

If you mix its food yourself, you can easily give your dog too much in terms of vitamins and minerals, which can also be bad for your dog's health. You can avoid these problems by giving it ready-made food of a good brand. These products are well balanced and contain everything your dog needs. Supplements such as vitamin preparations are superfluous. The amount of food your dog needs depends on its weight and activity level. You can find guidelines on the packaging. Split the food into two meals per day if possible and always ensure there is a bowl of fresh drinking water next to its food.

Give your dog the time to digest its food; do not let it outside straight after a meal. A dog should also never play on a full stomach. This can cause bloat (gastric torsion): because of excessive gas content the stomach becomes overstretched. This can be fatal for your dog.

Because the nutritional needs of a dog depend, among other things, on its age and way of life, there are many different types of dog food available. There are light foods for less active dogs, energy foods for working dogs and senior foods for the older dog.

Dry puppy foods
There is a wide assortment of puppy chunks on the market. These chunks contain a higher content of growth-promoting nutrients, such as protein and calcium. For large breeds such as the Boxer there are special puppy chunks for larger breeds available. Other puppy chunks for smaller dogs may promote growth too fast and can cause conditions such as hip and elbow-dysplasia (see chapter Health). Give your puppy only special puppy chunks for larger breeds.

Canned foods, mixer and dry foods

Ready-made foods available at pet shops or in the supermarket can roughly be split into canned food, mixer and dry food. Whichever form you choose, ensure that it is a complete food with all the necessary ingredients. You can see this on the packaging.

Most dogs love canned food. Although the better brands are composed well, they do have one disadvantage: they are soft. A dog fed only on canned food will not benefit from the gently abrasive effects of dry food and may potentially more quickly develop problems such as plaque, and/or periodontitis. Besides canned food, give your dog hard foods at certain times or a chew especially designed for the oral care of your dog.

Mixer is a food consisting of chunks, dried vegetables and grains. Almost all moisture has been extracted. The advantages of mixer are that it is light and keeps well. You add a certain amount of water and the meal is ready.
A disadvantage is that it must definitely not be fed without water. Without the extra fluid, mixer will absorb the fluids present in the stomach, with serious results. Should your dog manage to get at the bag of mixer or dry chunks and enjoy its contents, give the dog small amounts of water – half a cup – over short time (20 – 30 minutes) intervals.
Dry chunks have also had the moisture extracted but not as much as mixer.
The advantage of dry foods is that they are hard, forcing the dog to crunch, removing plaque and massaging the gums.

Dog chew products

Of course, once in a while you want to spoil your dog with something extra. Do not give it bits of cheese or sausage as these contain too much salt and fat. There are various products available that a dog will find delicious and which are also healthy, especially for its teeth. You will find a large range of varying quality in the pet shop.

The butcher's left-overs

The bones of slaughtered animals have traditionally been given to the dog and dogs are crazy about them, but they are not without risks. Pork and poultry bones are weak. They can splinter and cause serious injury to the intestines. Beef bones are more suitable, but they must first be cooked to kill off dangerous bacteria. Pet shops carry a range of smoked, cooked and dried abattoir left-overs, such as pigs' ears, bull penis, tripe sticks, oxtails, gullet, dried muscle meat, and hoof chews.

Fresh meat

If you do want to give your dog fresh meat occasionally, never give it raw, but always boiled or roasted. Raw or not fully cooked pork or chicken can contain life-threatening organisms. Chicken can be contaminated by the notorious salmonella bacteria, while pork can carry the Aujeszky virus. This disease is incurable and will quickly lead to the death of your pet.

Little shoes made from buffalo hide

Buffalo or cowhide chews

Dog chews are mostly made of cowhide or buffalo hide.
Chews are usually knotted or pressed hide and can come in the form of little shoes, twisted sticks, lollies, balls and various other shapes; nice to look at and a nice change.

Munchy sticks

Munchy sticks

Munchy sticks are green, yellow, red or brown coloured sticks of various thicknesses. They consist of ground buffalo hide with a number of often undefined additives. Dogs usually love them because these sticks have been dipped in the blood of slaughtered animals. The composition and quality of these between-meal treats is not always clear. Some are fine, but some have been found to contain high levels of cardboard and even paint residues. Choose a product with clearly described ingredients.

Something to drink

A dog can go days without eating if it must, but definitely not without drinking! Make sure it always has a bowl of fresh water available. Food and water bowls of stainless steel are the easiest to keep clean.

Overweight?

Recent investigations have shown that many dogs are overweight. A dog usually gets too fat because of over-feeding and lack of exercise. Medicines or disease are rarely the cause. Dogs that get too fat are often given too much food or too many treats between meals. Gluttony or boredom can also be a cause, and a dog often puts on weight following neutering or spaying. Due to changes in hormone levels, it becomes less active and consumes less energy. Finally, simply too little exercise alone can lead to a dog becoming overweight.

You can use the following rule of thumb to check whether your dog is overweight: you should be able to feel its ribs, but not see them. If you cannot feel its ribs then your dog is much too fat. Overweight dogs live a passive life; they play too little and tire quickly. They also suffer from all kinds of medical problems (problems with joints and the heart for example). They usually die younger too.

So it is important to make sure your dog does not get too fat. Always follow the guidelines on food packaging. Adapt them if your dog is less active or gets lots of snacks. Try to make sure your dog gets plenty of exercise by playing and running with it as much as you can. If your dog starts to show signs of putting on weight you can switch to a low-calorie food. If it is really too fat and reducing its food quantity does not help, then a special diet is the only solution.

Care

Good daily care is extremely important for your dog. A well cared-for dog is less likely to become ill. Caring for your dog is not only necessary but also a pleasure. Master and dog are paying each other some attention, and it is an excellent opportunity for a game and a cuddle.

The coat

Caring for your dog's coat involves regular brushing and combing, together with checking for parasites such as fleas. How often a dog needs to be brushed and combed depends on the length of its coat.

Bullmastiffs are less demanding in this respect. A shorthaired dog needs very little maintenance outside the moulting season. A healthy Bullmastiff has a shiny coat, which should be brushed once a week with a rubber massage brush. It is advisable to get a puppy used to being brushed from an early age, and to brush it every day, as 'Start them young!' applies to dogs too.

Brushing your dog every week should make bathing superfluous. If, however, your dog had a good roll in something unpleasant, then wash it with a special dog shampoo. The acidity level of your dog's skin is different to that of human skin.

Especially during the moulting period (twice a year), you should give your Bullmastiff's coat a stiff brushing everyday. This is essential: brushing promotes the growth of the new coat and prevents your furniture being buried under dog's hairs. Brush in the direction the coat is growing, but also in the opposite direction. Keep on brushing until no more loose hairs come out of the coat. Use the right equipment for taking care of the coat. Combs should not be too sharp and you should use a rubber or natural hair brush.

If you get a puppy used to being brushed from an early age, it will enjoy having its coat cared for. Only bathe a dog when it is really necessary, as shampoo removes fat from the skin and coat. A Bullmastiff should never need to be washed, but should your dog have managed to enjoy a wonderful roll in a cow-pat, then it is time for a good scrub.

Always use a special dog shampoo and make sure it does not get into the dog's eyes or ears. Rinse the suds out thoroughly and only let your dog outside again when it is completely dry. Even dogs can catch a cold.

A vet can prescribe special medicinal shampoos for some skin problems. Always follow the instructions to the letter.

Good flea prevention is highly important to avoid skin and coat problems. Fleas must be treated not only on the dog itself but also in its surroundings (see the chapter on parasites). Coat problems can also occur due to an allergy to certain food substances. In such cases, a vet can prescribe a hypo-allergenic diet.

Skin folds
The skin folds under the eyes need to be cleaned regularly. To prevent infections it is important to keep the skin folds dry. Spend enough attention to this, because these infections are very uncomfortable for your dog.

Eyes

A dog's eyes should be cleaned regularly. Discharge gets into the corners of the eye. You can easily remove it by wiping it downward with your thumb. If you do not like doing that, use a piece of tissue or toilet paper.

Keeping your dog's eyes clean will take only a few seconds a day, so do it every day. If the discharge becomes yellow this could point to an irritation or infection. Eye drops (from your vet) will quickly solve this problem.

Ears

The ears are often forgotten when caring for dogs. They must be checked at least once a week. If the ears of your dog are very dirty or show too much wax, you must clean them. This should be done preferably with a clean cotton cloth, moistened with lukewarm water or baby oil. Cotton wool is not suitable due to the fluff it can leave behind. NEVER enter the ear canal with an object. If you neglect cleaning your dog's ears there is a substantial risk of infection. A dog that is constantly scratching at its ears might be suffering from dirty ears, an ear infection or ear mites, making a visit to the vet essential.

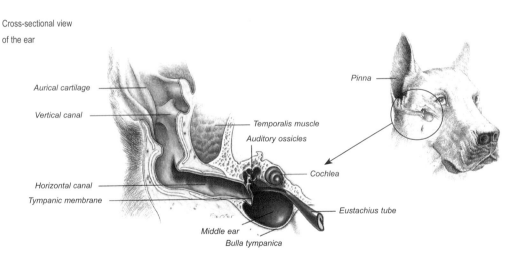

Cross-sectional view of the ear

Aurical cartilage
Vertical canal
Pinna
Temporalis muscle
Auditory ossicles
Cochlea
Horizontal canal
Tympanic membrane
Eustachius tube
Middle ear
Bulla tympanica

Nails

On a dog that regularly walks on hard surfaces, the nails usually grind themselves down. In this case there is no need to clip its nails. But it would not do any harm to check their length now and again, especially on Bullmastiffs that do not get out on the street very often. Using a piece of paper, you can easily see whether its nails are too long. If you can push the paper between the nail and the ground when the dog is standing, then the nail has the right length.

Nails that are too long can bother a dog. It can injure itself when scratching, so they must be kept trimmed. You can buy special nail clippers in pet shops. Be careful not to clip back too far as you could cut into the quick, which can bleed profusely.
If you feel unsure, have this important task done by a vet or an animal groom.
Special attention is needed for the dewclaw, i.e. the nail on the inside of the hind leg.
Clip this nail back regularly, otherwise it can get caught and become damaged.

Anal glands

When a dog sits on its bum and tries to move forward by using only its forelegs (called scooting), then you can be sure that its anal glands are bothering it. The anal sacs can be found on the left and right side of the anus. In case these sacs are full they start itching and cause pain to the dogs. The dog tries to bite them and if you do not notice it immediately, your dog will bite them completely open. You can prevent this by squeezing them out. However, if you do not know how to do this, please go to a veterinarian to solve this problem. You can also visit a professional dog groom.

Teeth

A Bullmastiff generally has few problems with its teeth, although it might suffer from tartar and bad breath when it gets older. To prevent this, you should have the teeth checked for tartar when taking your dog to the veterinarian for its annual vaccinations. Bad breath can be the result of dental problems.

Bad breath can also be caused by stomach problems or certain foods. It is then advisable to switch to a different diet.

A dog must be able to eat properly to stay in good condition, so it needs healthy teeth. Check its teeth regularly. If you suspect that something is not well, contact your vet. Regular feeds of hard dry food can help keep your dog's teeth clean and healthy. There are special dog chews on the market that help prevent plaque and help keep the animal's breath fresh. What really helps is to brush the teeth of your dog regularly.

You can use special toothbrushes for dogs, but a finger wrapped in a small piece of gauze will also do the job. Get your dog used to having its teeth cleaned at an early age and you will have no problems.

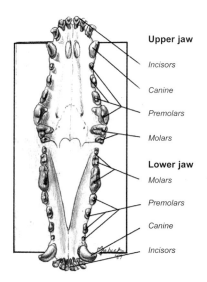

Schematic representation of the teeth

Upper jaw

Incisors

Canine

Premolars

Molars

Lower jaw

Molars

Premolars

Canine

Incisors

Left: profile of the teeth

Right: front view of the teeth

Toothpaste for humans should not be used for dogs, because it contains fluoride. When brushing the teeth of your dog, it might swallow down some toothpaste, which might cause it to vomit. It is best to buy special dog toothpaste. This toothpaste has a pleasant taste for dogs and dogs therefore easily accept it.

You can even teach an older dog to have its teeth cleaned. With a dog chew as a reward it will soon get used to it.

Dental Plaque and strong breath

Dental care and a fresh breath are very normal for human beings. However, this is not so natural for our dogs. Although the dog-owners get more and more aware of the fact that dental care is important for dogs as well, there still are many dogs that have a strong breath because of dental plaque or tartar.

In the first place, tartar is the cause of gingivitis, which spreads more and more and in the long run this even can cause problems to heart, kidneys and liver. So dental care is no redundant luxury!

The function of microbes

It is quite normal to have many microbes in the mouth. After every meal a thin layer of food stays behind on the teeth, which is a good breeding ground for microbes. All this together is called dental plaque. The degradation products from microbes are acidic and they damage the teeth. As a result of this, gingivitis and paradontitis are formed and as a consequence of that the dog might even lose its teeth. In addition to this it gets more and more difficult to clean the teeth when there is irregular dental care. The fact is that dental plaque will turn hard as time goes by and then it is called tartar. Tartar can be removed by the veterinarian while the dog will be anaesthetized.

Paradontitis

Dogs fortunately have less problems with cavities. However, paradontitis is the most frequent dental problem among dogs. When a dog has this dental problem, the gums, the teeth and the dental alveolus will become affected by microbes in the mouth of the dog.

More than 80% of all adult pets older than three years find themselves in the different stages of this dental problem, and have suffered from a strong breath, pain and/or loss of teeth. In the long run, the microbes from the mouth can come into the blood and damage several important organs!

Special feeding

Your veterinarian can prescribe your dog a special diet-food. This food can help your dog in two different ways. First by mechanical cleaning of the teeth through the special form, size and shape of the chunks. By eating this kind of food, the teeth are cleaned and it will prevent that plaque and tartar are built up.

The second way is by adding ingredients that prevent the transformation of plaque into tartar and that also prevents a strong breath.

Additivo in drinking water

Nowadays it is possible to add a tasty additive to the drinking water in order to prevent plaque, tartar and strong breath with dogs. This anti-plaque liquid can simply be added to the drinking water of th dog. This product contains the active substances chloro hexidine and xylitol, which restrain the increase of microbes in the mouth and because of that they prevent the building up of plaque. Apart from that, xylitol restrains the building up of tartar and takes care of a fresh breath.

So every time that your dog drinks, the teeth are automatically taken care of. Refresh the drinking water every day, even if there is some water left.

Regular check ups by the veterinarian

Apart from the daily dental care at home, it is advisable to have a regular check up by the veterinarian. Gingivitis and other dental problems can be found in time. Dogs can hide their dental problems very well! Your veterinarian will clean the teeth of your pet in a very professional way and he also has the right dental care products.

Rearing

It is very important that your dog is well brought up and obedient. This not only makes it more fun for you to be with your dog, but it also makes it more pleasant for other people.
A puppy can learn in a playful manner what it must and must not do.

Praise and consistency are two very important tools when bringing up a dog. When you reward your puppy for good behaviour with your voice, a pat or something tasty, it will soon learn to be obedient. A puppy course can be very helpful here.

When dealing with your dog, it is also useful to know something about the life of dogs, i.e. wolves, in the wild.

In the wild, wolves, the ancestors of our dogs, live in packs. They are therefore used to living in a group. Our domestic dogs view their families as their packs. In fact, our dogs see us as dogs, too. Every pack has a hierarchy. This means that there is one boss, the alpha animal, and all the other animals are ranked according to importance, right to the lowest position, the omega animal. There is a constant battle for the alpha spot in the pack. When you take a dog into your home, it is therefore very important to make it clear where its place is in the family. This is simply done by following twelve rules. In this chapter, we deal with the 'rules of the pack', what they are, how you can apply them and what you can do and what you should not do.

The rules of the pack

Rule 1
The Alpha dog sleeps where it wants and no-one is to approach it.
An animal high up in the hierarchy can choose its own place to rest. This place is always respected by the animals lower in the hierarchy. If an inferior animal comes close to a superior animal which is resting, the latter will growl to make it clear that the inferior animal must not approach.

If the inferior animal approaches anyway, there is a real risk that the superior animal will bite. This rule not only applies to resting and sleeping. The superior animal always has access to places which are prohibited to the inferior animal.

The alpha animal is therefore not always the 'official' pack leader; it is the animal highest in the hierarchy present at that moment.

Advice:
* Never let your dog sleep on your bed
* The bedroom should actually be entirely forbidden territory for your dog.
* You can also prohibit access to other parts of the house. This makes it clear to the dog that you are higher in the hierarchy.
* If your dog lies on a chair which you want to sit on, simply sit down without saying anything. If necessary, sit on your dog.

Don't
* Never try to take away your dog's safe place.
* Never let your dog take away your place.
* Never let your dog refuse people access to certain places.

Rule 2
The alpha male has the highest position.
In a pack of dogs, you can often see that the pack leader lies somewhat higher than the rest of the pack, as if he wants to have a good overview over the pack. The alpha male thus demonstrates his high position. Domestic dogs also often want to lie on a somewhat higher place and they might try to climb onto the headrest of your sofa in an attempt to demonstrate that they have a high position. Dogs which are lower down in the hierarchy would never dare to demonstrate such behaviour. Dogs demonstrate what position they hold within the pack not just by lying on a higher place, but also with their general attitude.

Advice
- When you notice that your dog wants to lie on a higher position while you are present, do not allow it.
- If, for example you are sitting on the stairs and your dog comes to sit with you, make sure that it does not sit on a higher step than you do.

Don't
- Never let your dog crawl onto your lap without permission.
- Never pick up your dog to a higher position in the presence of another dog (or human), as this will give your dog an artificial and undeserved higher position.

Rule 3

The alpha male eats first. The others get the left-overs, unless the alpha decides to keep everything for himself.

When the pack has caught a large prey, it is not necessarily divided up democratically. The alpha animal always eats first, possibly together with the alpha bitch at most. The rest of the pack must wait until the leader has finished.

The alpha male will decide when the rest of the pack gets its food. He might also decide that the others do not get anything at all. In this case, he simply puts the remains of the prey somewhere else and moves away. In fact, the alpha animal challenges the inferior animals to take the food. If an inferior animal dares to approach the food, the alpha animal will growl loudly and bite the inferior animal in the neck to correct it, or grab the food away from it to display his higher position.

Advice

- Prepare your dog's food and place it out of reach. Then you go and have dinner first.
  Only feed your dog when the whole family has finished. Preferably, first give the 'stay' command and then allow your dog to approach its food.
- Place toys on the floor close to your dog. When it wants to take the toy, you grab it away. Repeat this a few times. Your dog will soon stop trying to take the toy. This is the moment when your dog acknowledges your superiority.

Don't

- Never feed your dog anything while the family is having dinner. This gives the dog the same position in the hierarchy as the members of the family.
- Be careful with food envy! Never take food away from your dog and stay away from its food bowl when it is eating.

Food envy

Many dogs refuse to give up things they carry in their mouth (food, toys). If you do try to take these things from your dog, it will growl. We can often see the same behaviour in dogs that are eating. When you approach your dog's bowl, it will growl. This behaviour is called 'food envy'.

Rule 4

Playing, not fighting, is the way to establish hierarchy.
A dog can determine and confirm hierarchical positions during play. For young dogs, in particular, playing is also a way to learn to live in a group, and to slowly find out which position they will have within the pack.

Our pet dogs no longer live according to the harsh laws of nature. This allows them to remain playful to an old age. The only reason for dogs to live in a pack is because this increases their chances of success when hunting.

If they would constantly fight to determine or confirm their position in the hierarchy, there would be a lot of casualties and an injured animal is no help when hunting. We therefore more often see dogs play than fight to establish the hierarchy. After all, their life partly depends on the health of the others in the pack. When two strange dogs walk past each other, they will sometimes have a go at each other. As they are not members of the same pack, this has nothing to do with establishing a hierarchy, but with protecting their territory.

Territory

The territory is the domain of the pack. This territory may be several kilometres across and is divided into three different 'sectors'. In the outer circle of the territory, pack members will make it clear to intruders that they must stay out. If an intruder manages to get into the middle circle, the pack will attack him. However, he will be given the chance to escape during this attack. The innermost circle is the centre of the pack. The puppies stay there and the entire pack retreats to this sector to rest. Defending this place is a matter of life and death. If we look at how closely humans live to each other in the Western world, it is not surprising that dogs have so many territorial conflicts. A dog will, after all, not be satisfied with its own garden. Its territory is much bigger. The garden is simply the centre of the territory. The rest is outside your garden fence. This means that the territories of dogs which live closely together overlap each other. Even when walking a dog on the lead, it still has a territory. It is a mobile territory, and the dog sees itself as the centre. It is therefore not surprising that two dogs often have a go at each other when taken out for a walk. After all, the centre of the territory must be defended fanatically.

Advice

- Always keep games under control: you determine the course of a game, not your dog.
- When you are playing with your dog, you must be aware that it constantly tries to get over you in the hierarchy. Therefore constantly pay attention to this rule. If you think that your dog is trying to dominate the game, stop immediately and ignore it completely for a while.

Don't

- Never let your dog dominate retrieve or tug-of-war games.
- Never let your dog determine how or what you are going to play. That is your decision.

Rule 5

The alpha wins each and every game.

When dogs are playing, you can see that a superior animal will always assume a higher position than an inferior animal. The superior animal will decide when the game is over and it will always win.

Advice

Make sure that you always win the last game when playing with your dog. It is possible to let your dog win a game once in a while, but you must dominate the major part of it. How many games your dog is allowed to win depends on the hierarchical relationship between you and your dog. A dominant dog should never be allowed to win. A submissive dog can be allowed to feel like a winner once in a while.

Don't

- Never let your dog win the last game.
- Never finish a retrieve game by throwing the object. The dog will pick up the object and therefore in fact be the winner of the game. A tug-of-war game with a rope must not be finished by letting go of the rope and giving it to the dog. Take the rope and put it away.

Rule 6
Each pack member makes place for the highest in rank.
If a superior animal goes somewhere, all the inferior animals will move out of its way. The superior animal will go in a straight line, without swerving, to the place it wants to go. No other dog will stand in its way. Only inferior animals will move aside.

Don't
- If your dog is coming towards you and wants to move past you, do not move aside.
- Never swerve around your dog if you want to go past it. And do not step over it, even when it is asleep.

Rule 7
The highest in the hierarchy will always go through a narrow passageway first.
A narrow passageway is a very wide term in this context. It is not only a doorway or a gate, but it can also be the alleyway between two houses, the space between parked cars or even a forest path.

The clearest example for this rule is a pack of hunting dogs. When these dogs are let out of their kennels, it is always the animal highest in the hierarchy which exits first. Dogs often run ahead when out on a walk. They do this to confirm their higher position in comparison to their owner.

Advice
- Open a door a little. If your dog wants to go through, close it. Be very careful that your dog's nose does not get caught, however! Repeat this until your dog no longer attempts to go through the door. Then go through the door yourself and let your dog follow you.
- Sometimes your dog will try to go ahead of you through a passageway, which cannot be closed with a door or gate. In this case, keep your dog on a four to five metre long lead. Walk towards the passageway. If your dog wants to go ahead, turn around and walk away from the passageway. If your dog does not follow straight away, it will get a sudden pull when the lead tightens. It should now follow you. Repeat these steps until your dog no longer shows the intention of going through the passageway first.

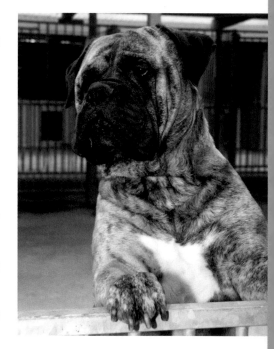

Don't
- You must never try to physically prevent a dog from going through a passageway first. There is no point in forcing your dog physically to accept you as a leader. If you try to stop your dog in such a manner, it will soon learn that it simply has to be faster than you. This way, the dog tries to prevent you stopping it.
- Never let your dog pull on the lead when walking it.

Rule 8
Each pack member pays respect to the alpha male every day
All dogs in a pack confirm their submissive position every day by consistently applying the rules of the pack. They devote most of their time to the alpha dog, which they honour. This becomes clear in their greetings, for example. First the highest in the hierarchy is greeted, and then the other members according to their status. Everything that happens in a pack reflects the movement from top to bottom. Inferior animals always respect superior animals.

Advice
- Respect all the rules of the pack every day.
- Always respect the hierarchy.
- Always show respect for those superior (for children, this is the parents).
- When eating, when wiping your feet after a walk or when going through a passageway, make sure that you always come first and that your dog always comes last.
- Always greet the highest members of the hierarchy first, and the lower members after that. This means that a dog must be greeted last.

Don't
- It is absolutely wrong to act against the hierarchy. According to the rules of the pack, a superior animal must never let an inferior animal have an advantage.
  It is therefore very confusing for your dog, if, for example, you greet it before you greet the other members of the family.

Rule 9
The alpha dog decides what is best.
The pack leader decides everything that goes on within a pack. He decides when to sleep, when to hunt, when to play, when to eat, etc. No other dog within the pack will make decisions which contradict those of the leader.

Advice
- As the boss, you make all the decisions for your dog within the human/dog pack. You decide when your dog is allowed to go for a walk, to eat, play and sleep.

Don't
- Never let your dog decide. Therefore do not follow its demand (begging) to go for a walk or to play with it. You alone decide when you do anything with your dog.

Rule 10

An inferior member of the pack pays attention to the alpha.

A superior animal never approaches an inferior animal, unless it wants to reprimand it.
An inferior animal always approaches a superior animal, and assumes a submissive posture (head low, ears back, tail low). This is called active submission. A superior animal may approach an inferior animal to reprimand it. In this case, the superior animal will assume a superior posture (dominance).

Active submission

Inferior dogs sometimes approach superior dogs. In this case, they assume a low posture: the ears are pinned back, the tail is carried low and the body is generally held somewhat lower towards the ground. When an inferior animal reaches the superior animal, it will lick the corners of its mouth. This is a social gesture which dogs inherited from their ancestors. With this gesture, the inferior dog confirms the superior dog in its status. We call this active submission: the inferior dog initiates the submission.

Passive submission

In the case of passive submission, the inferior animal also assumes a low posture. The only difference is that this time the superior animal initiates the submission. When it approaches the inferior animal with a superior posture, the inferior animal will react immediately and assume an inferior posture. If it does not do this, it will be reprimanded by the superior animal.

Advice

• Always make your dog approach you.
• Regularly play chase games, where your dog must follow you.
• Only ever approach your dog when you need to reprimand it.

Don't

• Never approach your dog. Particularly not when it is lying in its safe place. The dog wants to have some peace and quiet here. When approaching your dog, you are moving for it and a superior animal never moves for an inferior animal!

Rule 11
Only the alpha animal has the right to ignore.
A superior animal will often ignore the inferior animal when it passes by. An inferior animal would never dare to ignore a superior dog in such a way, it would be punished immediately. In general, a pack leader will usually ignore the lowest members of the pack.

It is also not his job to watch over the entire pack, as this would require far too much energy. Every member of the pack therefore needs to pay attention to the alpha animal. The group thus stays together: where the alpha animal leads, the rest follows.

Advice
• Regularly ignore your dog when passing by.
  This shows it that you are still higher up in the hierarchy.
• When your dog is importunately demanding your attention or jumping up at you, it is best to ignore it completely. Ignoring it is punishment for your dog. Dogs would rather have negative attention than no attention at all. If you shout at your dog for jumping up at you, you are actually paying attention to it, which is exactly what it wants.

Don't
• Never let your dog ignore you. If necessary, demand its attention or motivate it so that it becomes interested in you again.

Rule 12

A superior animal has the right to allow privileges.

Both with humans and with dogs, we often see that someone who is high up in the hierarchy often deals out privileges to the ones directly below. The lower animal can in turn hand out privileges to the one below it. An animal will never hand out more privileges than it received.

This means that the lowest animal in the hierarchy will have the least privileges of all. Privileges which have been handed out can also be withdrawn. If an animal does not behave exceptionally well, it could easily lose all its privileges.

Advice

• Once you have established the hierarchy within your human/dog pack with the help of the above rules, you can give your dog some privileges. In other words: you may decide to apply some of the rules less strictly. You need to realize that such privileges allow your dog to move a little closer to the rest of the family in terms of hierarchy. Therefore never give your dog too much freedom. Make sure that there is still enough distance in the hierarchy between your dog and the rest of the family.

• You may hand out privileges, but you do not have to!

Don't

• Never allow a dog privileges that are not far enough below those of all the other members of the pack. It will soon take advantage.

(Dis)obedience

Bullmastiffs are intelligent dogs. Never listen to anyone telling you that Bullmastiffs will never listen and are too stubborn to learn anything. A Bullmastiff will do anything for you, as long as it considered it carefully first. You cannot yell at your Bullmastiff if you want it to obey, but you must encourage it with an enthusiastic voice. Make it feel that it is an honour for it to do something for you. There are Bullmastiffs that have achieved the highest obedience diplomas with the help of their enthusiastic owners.

A dog that does not want to obey you is not just a problem for you, but also for your surroundings. It is therefore important to avoid unwanted behaviour. In fact, this is what training your dog is all about, so get started early. 'Start them young!' applies to dogs too. An untrained dog is not just a nuisance, but can also cause dangerous situations by running into the road, chasing joggers or jumping at people.

A dog must be trained out of this undesirable behaviour as quickly as possible. The longer you let it go on, the more difficult it will become to correct it. The best thing to do is to attend a special obedience course. This can help to correct the dog's behaviour, as well as helping the owner to learn how to handle undesirable behaviour at home. A dog must not only obey its master during training, but everywhere and at any time.

Always be consistent when training good behaviour and correcting annoying behaviour. Reward the dog for good behaviour and never punish it after the event for any wrongdoing. This means: If your dog finally comes after you have been calling it a long time, then reward it. If you are angry because you had to wait so long, it may feel it is actually being punished for coming. It will probably not obey at all the next time for fear of punishment.

Try to take no notice of undesirable behaviour. Your dog will perceive your reaction (even a negative one) as a reward for this behaviour. If you need to correct the dog, then do this immediately. Use your voice or grip it by the scruff of its neck and push it to the ground. This is the way a mother dog calls her pups to order. Rewards for good behaviour are, by far, preferable to punishment; they always get a better result.

House-training

The very first training and one of the most important that a dog needs is house-training. The basis for good house-training is keeping a good eye on your puppy. If you pay attention, you will notice that it always sniffs or turns around the same place before doing its business there. Pick it up gently and place it outside, always at the same place. Reward it abundantly if it does its business there.

Always put a puppy out at the same times: In the morning as soon as it is awake, before and after meals, every time it has been asleep or has been playing, and in the evenings before bedtime. It will quickly learn the meaning, especially if it is rewarded with a dog biscuit for a successful attempt. Let it relieve itself before playing with it, otherwise it will forget to do so and you will not reach your goal.

Of course, it is not always possible to go out after every snack or snooze.

Lay newspapers at different spots in the house. Whenever the pup needs to do its business, place it on a newspaper. After some time it will start to look for a place itself. Then start to reduce the number of newspapers until there is just one left, at the front or back door. The puppy will learn to go to the door if it needs to relieve itself. Then you put it on the lead and go out with it. Finally you can remove the last newspaper. Your puppy is now house-trained.

One thing that certainly will not work is punishing an accident after the event. A dog whose nose is rubbed in its urine or its stool will not understand that at all. It will only get frightened of you. Rewarding works much better than punishment. An indoor kennel or cage can be a good tool to help in house-training.

A puppy will not foul its own spot, so an indoor kennel can be a good solution for the night, or during periods during the day when you cannot watch it.
A kennel must not become a prison where the dog is locked up day and night.

First exercises

To get the right result it is important to be clear and consistent during training. Commands should be short and clear, like 'Lie down!' or 'Stay there!'. Commands should always be in the same tone and must be clearly different from one-another.

Be consistent once you have chosen the commands. If you want the dog to lie down, it is no use using 'Lie down!' once and 'Lay!' the next time. Once the dog has understood the intention, it should only be necessary to call a command once, clearly and in a certain tone. Repeating a command actually makes your dog disobedient. If it does not react immediately, make a disapproving sound while walking towards it. Shouting usually does not have the desired result. Dogs have exceptional hearing, much better than a human's. Commands should be given in a quiet and preferably soft tone. Keep raising your voice for exceptional situations.

The basic commands for an obedient dog are those for *sit*, *lie down*, *come* and *stay*. But a puppy should first learn its name. Use it as much as possible from the first day on, followed by a friendly 'Here'. Reward it with your voice and a pat when it comes to you. Your puppy will quickly recognise the intention and has now learned its first command in a playful manner. Do not appear too strict towards a young puppy; do not always punish it immediately if it does not always react in the right way. When you call your puppy to you in this way, have it come right to you.

You can teach a pup to *sit* by holding a piece of dog biscuit above its nose and then slowly moving it backwards. The puppy's head will also move backwards until its hind legs slowly go down. At that moment you say 'Sit!'. Use your free hand to gently push the hindquarters down. After a few attempts, it will quickly know this nice game. Use the 'Sit!' command before you give your dog its food, put it on understand lead or before it is allowed to cross the street.

Teaching the command to get the dog to *lie down* is similar. Instead of moving the piece of dog biscuit backwards, move it down vertically until your hand reaches the ground and then forwards. The dog will also move its forepaws forwards and lie down on its own. Again, help it with your free hand. Then say 'Lie down!' or 'Lay!'. *Lying down* is useful when you want a dog to be quiet.

Two people are needed for the '*Come!*' command. One holds the dog back while the other runs away. After about fifteen metres, he or she stops and enthusiastically calls 'Come!'. The other person now lets the dog go, and it should obey the command at once. Again you reward it abundantly. The '*Come!*' command is useful in many situations and good for safety too.

A dog learns to *stay* from the sitting or lying position. While it is sitting or lying down, you call the command 'Stay!' and then step back one step. If the dog moves with you, quietly put it back in position, without displaying anger. If you do react angrily, you are actually punishing it for coming, and you'll only confuse your dog. It cannot understand that coming is rewarded one time, and punished another. Once the dog stays nicely, reward it abundantly. Do not let it lay more than a few seconds in the beginning. Once it understands what is expected, you can make the time longer, and increase the distance between you and the dog at the same time.
The '*stay*' command is useful, for example, when getting out of the car.

Go up and down the stairs
Young dogs still have a lot of cartilage and their skeleton as well as their joints still experience quite some growth. For that reason they are not allowed to walk up and down the stairs before they are at least one year old. This means that you have to carry your dog up and down the stairs yourself.
Even if the dog wants to walk up and down the stairs by itself, you have to forbid it to do so.

Courses
Because it is important that a Bullmastiff is properly brought up, we recommend that you attend an obedience course with your dog. Obedience courses to help you bring up your dog are available across the country.
These courses are not just informative, but also fun for dog and master.

With a puppy, you can begin with a puppy course. This is designed to provide the basic training. A puppy that has attended such a course has learned about all kinds of things that it will confront in later life: other dogs, humans, traffic and what these mean.

The puppy will also learn obedience and to follow a number of basic commands. Apart from all that, attention will be given to important subjects such as brushing, being alone, travelling in a car, and doing its business on the right places.

The next step after a puppy course is a course for young dogs. This course repeats the basic exercises and ensures that the growing dog does not get into bad habits. After this, the dog can move on to an obedience course for full-grown dogs. For more information on where to find courses in your area, contact your local kennel club. You can get the address from The Kennel Club of Great Britain in London. In some areas, the RSPCA organises obedience classes and your local branch may be able to give you information.

Play and toys

There are various ways to play with your dog. You can romp and run with it, but also play a number of games, such as retrieving, tug-of-war, hide-and-seek and catch. Bullmastiffs love this kind of games. A tennis ball is ideal for retrieving; and you can play tug-of-war with an old sock or a special tugging rope. Play tug-of-war only when your dog is at least one year old. A puppy must first get its second teeth and then they need several months to strengthen.

If you start too young, there is a real chance of your dog's teeth becoming deformed. You can use almost anything for a game of hide-and-seek. A frisbee is ideal for catching games. Never use too small a ball for games. It can easily get lodged into the dog's throat.

Play is extremely important. Not only does it strengthen the bond between dog and master, but it is also healthy for both. Make sure that you are the one that ends the game. Only stop when the dog has brought back the ball or frisbee, and make sure you always win the tug-of-war. This confirms your dominant position in the hierarchy. Use the toys only during play so that the dog does not forget their significance. When choosing a special dog toy, remember that dogs are hardly careful with them. So always buy toys of good quality that a dog cannot easily destroy.

Be very careful with sticks and twigs. The latter, particularly, can easily splinter. A splinter of wood in your dog's throat or intestines can cause awful problems. Throwing sticks or twigs can also be dangerous. If they stick into the ground a dog can easily run into them with an open mouth.

Aggression

Bullmastiffs are normally practically never aggressive. However, it can happen that your dog will be less friendly towards other animals or people. It's therefore a good idea to understand a little about the background of aggression in dogs.

In general there are two different types of aggressive behaviour:
The anxious-aggressive dog and the dominant-aggressive dog. An anxious-aggressive dog can be recognised by its pulled back ears and its low position. It will have pulled in its lips, showing its teeth. This dog is aggressive because it is very frightened and feels cornered. It would prefer to run away, but if it cannot then it will bite to defend itself. It will grab its victim anywhere it can. The attack is usually brief and as soon as the dog can

see a way to escape, it is gone. In a confrontation with other dogs, it will normally turn out to be the loser. It can become even more aggressive once it has realised that people or other dogs are afraid of it. This behaviour cannot be corrected just like that. First you have to try and understand what the dog is afraid of. Professional advice is a good idea here. The wrong approach can easily make the problem worse.

The dominant-aggressive dog's body language is different. Its ears stand up and its tail is raised and stiff. This dog will always go for its victim's arms, legs or throat. It is extremely self-assured and highly placed in the dog hierarchy. Its attack is a display of power rather than a consequence of fear. This dog needs to know who is the boss. You must bring it up rigorously and with a strong hand. An obedience course can help.

A dog may also bite when it is in pain. This is a natural defensive reaction. In this case try to resolve the dog's fear as far as possible. Reward it for letting you get to the painful spot. Be careful, because a dog in pain may also bite its master! Muzzling it can help to prevent problems in case you have to do something that may be painful. Never punish a dog for this type of aggression!

Fear

The source of anxious behaviour can often be traced to the first weeks of a dog's life. A shortage of new experiences during the important socialisation phase has great influence on its later behaviour. A dog that never encountered humans, other dogs or animals during this period will be afraid of them later. This fear is common with Bullmastiffs brought up in a barn or kennel, with almost no contact with humans. As we saw, fear can lead to aggressive behaviour, so it is important that a puppy gets as many new impressions as possible in the first weeks of its life. Take it with you into town in the car or on the bus, walk with it down busy streets and allow it to have plenty of contact with humans, other dogs and other animals.

It is a huge task to turn an anxious, poorly socialised dog into a real pet. It will probably take an enourmous amount of attention, love, patience and energy to get this animal used to everything around it. Reward it often and give it plenty of time to adapt and, over time, it will learn to trust you and become less anxious. Try not to force anything, because this will always have the reverse effect. Here too, an obedience class can help a lot. A dog can be especially afraid of strangers. Have visitors give it something tasty as a treat. Put a can of dog biscuits by the door so that your visitors can spoil your dog when they arrive. Here again, do not try to force anything. If the dog is still frightened, leave it in peace.
Dogs are often frightened in certain situations; well-known examples are thunderstorms and fireworks. In these cases try to ignore their anxious behaviour.
If you react to a dog's whimpering and whining, it is the same as rewarding it. If you ignore its fear completely, the dog will quickly learn that nothing is wrong. You can speed up this 'learning process' by rewarding its positive behaviour.

Rewarding

Rewarding forms the basis for bringing up a dog. Rewarding good behaviour works far better than punishing bad behaviour and rewarding is also more fun than punishment. Over time the opinions on how to bring up dogs have gradually changed. In the past the proper way to correct bad behaviour was a sharp pull on the lead. Today, experts view rewarding as a positive incentive to get dogs to do what we expect of them. There are many ways to reward a dog. The usual ways are a pat or a friendly word, even without a tasty treat to go with it. Of course, a piece of dog biscuit does wonders when you are training a puppy. Be sure you always have something delicious in your pocket to reward good behaviour. Another form of reward is play. Whenever a dog notices that you have a ball in your pocket, it will not go far from your side. As soon as you have finished playing, put the ball away. In this way your dog will always do its best in exchange for a game.

Despite the emphasis you put on rewarding good behaviour, a dog can sometimes be a nuisance or disobedient. You must correct such behaviour immediately. Always be consistent; once 'no' must always mean 'no'.

Barking

Dogs which bark too much and too often are a nuisance for their surroundings. A dog-owner may tolerate barking up to a point, but neighbours are often annoyed by the unnecessary noise. Do not encourage your puppy to bark and yelp. Of course, it should be able to announce its presence, but if it goes on barking it must be called to order with a strict 'Quiet!'. If a puppy fails to obey, just hold its muzzle closed with your hand.

A dog will sometimes bark for long periods when left alone. It feels threatened and tries to get someone's attention by barking. There are special training programmes for this problem, where dogs learn that being alone is nothing to be afraid of, and that their master will always return.
You can practise this with your dog at home. Leave the room and come back in at once. Reward your dog if it stays quiet. Gradually increase the length of your absences and keep rewarding it as long as it remains quiet. Never punish the dog if it does bark or yelp. It will never understand punishment afterwards, and this will only make the problem worse. Never go back into the room as long as your dog is barking, as it will view this as a reward. You might want to make the dog feel more comfortable by switching the radio on for company during your absence. It will eventually learn that you always come back and the barking will reduce. If you do not get the required result, attend an obedience course or consult a behaviour therapist.

Breeding

Dogs, and thus also Bullmastiffs, follow their instincts, and reproduction is one of nature's important processes. For people who enjoy breeding dogs this is a positive circumstance.

Those who simply want a cosy companion however, do not need the regular adventures with females on heat and unrestrainable males.

Knowing a little about breeding dogs will help you to understand why they behave the way they do, and the measures you need to take when this happens.

Liability

Breeding dogs is more than simply 1+1= many. If you are planning to breed with your Bullmastiff, be on your guard, otherwise the whole affair can turn into a financial drama because, under the law, a breeder is liable for the quality of his puppies.

The kennel clubs place strict conditions on animals used for breeding (see the chapter "Health"). If you want to breed a litter for fun, but do not have the relevant experience, you can ask the breed association for advice. Be extremely careful, because, if the puppies you breed show any hereditary abnormalities in later life, you can be held liable by the new owners for any costs arising from any inherited defects. These (veterinary) costs can be enormous! So contact the breeder of your bitch or the breed association if you plan to breed a litter of Bullmastiffs.

The female in season

It is a myth that it is better for a bitch's health to produce a litter. It is better for most bitches not to have any young! Bitches become sexually mature at about eight to twelve months. Then they go into season for the first time.

They are on heat for two to three weeks. During the first ten days they discharge little drops of blood and they become steadily more attractive to males. The bitch is fertile during the second half of her season, and will accept a male to mate. The best time for mating is then between the tenth and thirteenth day of her season. A female's first season is often shorter and less severe than those that follow. If you do want to breed with your female you must allow this first and the second season to pass. Most bitches go into season twice per year.

If you do plan to breed with your Bullmastiff in the future, then spaying is not an option to prevent unwanted offspring. A temporary solution is a contraceptive injection, although this is controversial because of possible side effects such as womb infections and the possibility of mamilla tumours when the female gets older.

Phantom pregnancy

A phantom pregnancy is a not uncommon occurrence. The female behaves as if she has a litter. She takes all kinds of things to her basket and treats them like puppies. Her teats swell up and sometimes milk is actually produced. The female will sometimes behave aggressively towards humans or other animals, as if she is defending her young. Phantom pregnancies usually begin two months after a season and can last a number of weeks. If it happens to a bitch once, it will often then occur after every season.

If this is a problem, spaying is the best solution, because continual phantom pregnancies increase the risk of womb or teat conditions. In the short term a hormone treatment is worth trying, also perhaps giving the animal homeopathic medicines.

Camphor can give relief when teats are heavily swollen, but rubbing the teats with ice or a cold cloth (moisten and freeze) can also help relieve the pain. Feed the female less than usual, and make sure she gets enough attention and extra exercise.

Preparing to breed

If you do plan to breed a litter of puppies, you must first wait for your female to be physically and mentally full-grown. In any event you must let her first season pass. If you have a purebred Bullmastiff, then it certainly makes sense to mate her with the best possible candidate. Be meticulous with your preparations. As early as possible, some time before the bitch is expected to go into season, start the search for a potential mate. If your female is registered, and has passed all the health checks (see the chapter Health). The breeding club will help to find a suitable dog. It might also be a good idea to get in touch with the breeder of your Bullmastiff. This breeder knows his breeding lines best and probably knows which male is good to use for breeding your bitch. A good breeder knows all desired and undesired specialties about the breeding lines from his breed.

If you plan to mate your bitch with a dog not on The Kennel Club list, think about the following.

- Do not pick a dog without a pedigree.
- Let the owner confirm that he does not display any congenital defects.
- Observe the dog's character and temperament and look for characteristics that will reinforce the positive qualities of your bitch and compensate for any of her weak points or defective personality traits.
- Never breed two extremes together. If both parents are hyperactive, for example, there is a high chance that this (undesirable) trait will be even stronger in their offspring.

The owner of the dog will expect a certain amount as a cover fee. Sometimes a pup from the future litter may be the fee, in which case the owner of the male has the right of choosing first. Before mating your bitch, check that she is free of any parasites (external and internal). She must be fit, not overweight and vaccinated against all the usual diseases. If you want strong, healthy puppies, the mother-to-be must be in optimal condition. As soon as the female shows the first signs of being on heat, make an appointment with the owner of the male for the first mating attempt. In most cases, after the first apparently successful attempt at mating, the bitch is brought to the dog again after two or three days.

Think especially about the following: Accompanying a bitch through pregnancy, birth and the first eight to twelve weeks afterwards is a time-consuming affair. The first couple of weeks are a day-and-night job with the Bullmastiff! Never mate Bullmastiffs that have congenital defects.

Pregnancy

It is often difficult to tell at first when a bitch is pregnant. Only after about four weeks you can feel the pups in her womb. She will now slowly get fatter and her behaviour will usually change. Her teats will swell up during the last few weeks of pregnancy. The average pregnancy lasts 63 days, and costs the bitch more and more in terms of energy. In the beginning she should be fed her normal amount of food, but her nutritional needs increase in jumps during the second half of the pregnancy.

Give her approximately fifteen percent more food each week from the fifth week on. The mother-to-be needs extra energy and proteins during this phase of her pregnancy. (See chapter on feeding)

During the last weeks you can give her a concentrated food, rich in energy, such as dry puppy food. Divide this into several small portions per day, because she can no longer deal with large portions of food. Towards the end of the pregnancy, her energy needs can easily be one-and-a-half times more than usual.

After about seven weeks the mother will demonstrate nesting behaviour and begin to look for a place to give birth to her pups. This might be her own basket or a special birthing box. This must be ready at least one week before the birth to give the mother time to get used to it. The basket or box should preferably be in a quiet place.

Birth
A litter of Bullmastiff puppies counts five to eight puppies. Make sure that your vet knows when the birth is imminent. Normally Bullmastiffs give birth to their puppies without any problems. However when you are uncertain about this, you should always contact your veterinarian.

Suckling
After giving birth, the mother starts to produce milk. The suckling period is very demanding. During the first three to four weeks the pups rely entirely on their mother's milk. During this time she needs extra food and fluids. This can be up to three or four times the normal amount. If she's producing too little milk, you can give both the mother and her pups special puppy milk.

Here too, divide the high quantity of food the mother needs over several smaller portions. Again, choose a concentrated, high-energy, food and give her plenty of fresh drinking water, but not cow's milk, which can cause diarrhoea. You can start to give the pups some extra food from the third week. Start with specially designed starter food that matches very well with their mother's milk and can easily be eaten with the milk teeth from puppies. You start with one meal of starter food per week, which you gradually increase by one meal per week.

When the puppies are seven weeks old, they should be fully weaned, i.e. they no longer drink their mother's milk.
The mother's milk production gradually stops and her food needs also drop. Within a couple of weeks after weaning, the mother should again be getting the same amount of food as before the pregnancy.

When you feed your puppies, make sure that each pup gets its fair share. If you feel that one pup is missing out, set it apart when feeding but do this only as long as necessary and get it eating with its brothers and sisters as quickly as possible.

Only that way will it learn to fend for itself. Over-eating is just as dangerous as under-eating, so increase the amount gradually. Watch out for the growth and behaviour of the pups and regularly check that their stools are properly formed. Small hard stools can be a sign of malnutrition or lack of fluids. Stools that are too soft or runny are often caused by overfeeding.

Neutering and spaying

As soon as you are sure your bitch should never bear a (new) litter spaying is the best solution. During spaying, the uterus is surgically removed. The bitch no longer goes into season and can never become pregnant. The best age for a spaying is about eighteen months, when the bitch is more or less fully grown.

A male dog may also be neutered for medical reasons or to correct undesirable sexual behaviour. During neutering the testicles are removed, which is a simple procedure and usually without complications. There is no special age for neutering. Where possible, wait until the dog is fully grown.

Vasectomy is sufficient where it is only a case of making the dog infertile. In this case the dog keeps its sexual drive but can no longer reproduce.

Sport and show

Bullmastiffs will not be happy with just going round the block once in a while, especially when they are young. They will get bored and will start to behave badly at home.

If you want to keep your young Bullmastiff happy, you will have to do something with it!

Many kennel clubs run their own sports activities and championships. If you regularly participate in activities with your Bullmastiff, you will not only realise that the bond between master and dog has grown stronger, but also that your dog is quieter and more obedient at home.

Choosing a Bullmastiff as a companion needs serious consideration, and means that you must be prepared to meet its physical and psychological needs

Behaviour and obedience
You can pick from a whole range of obedience training courses, beginning with a puppy course. Bullmastiffs usually enjoy this type of course. Their strong will to please means they want to perform the exercises as well as possible. After elementary obedience courses, you can train your dog for various behaviour and obedience diplomas.

Obedience
You can follow up on basic obedience training by trying to pass the Behaviour and Obedience diplomas, classes 1, 2 & 3, with increasing degrees of difficulty.

This discipline is also practised in a competitive environment, and there are British, European and World Championships. Among other things, the dog must walk on the lead, follow at foot off the lead, stay standing or sit or lie for a set time while its master walks away and is out of sight for several minutes. Tracking and retrieving is trained and tested almost to perfection.

The British form of Obedience goes a step further; the accent here is on perfect performance of the set tasks. Highly intensive training is intended to make dog and master one unit, which, during the execution of several exercises, seems to be glued together. Obedience is only performed in competition, there are no diplomas.

Road safety

Road safety courses for dogs are especially useful. Here, your Bullmastiff can learn a few obedience exercises and at the end of the course can show you how safely it conducts itself in traffic.

Endurance

Once the dogs have learned to run next to the bicycle, they love doing this. It is also very good for the development of their muscles: the body moves nice and steady. In this way the muscles get stronger, without the vulnerable joints being overloaded. However, you must not have your Bullmastiff run next to your bicycle before it is at least one year old. Starting too early damages the development of its bones. Start slowly and make the distance longer bit by bit. It is never good to start too fast or to make a too long trip at the beginning.

NEVER go cycling when it is too warm. NEVER give your dog food before you go on a cycle-trip. And NEVER continue cycling too long.

Endurance is important for a Bullmastiff. After all, it is an active dog that needs plenty of exercise and space. During endurance training, the dog learns to trot (not run or gallop) beside a bicycle. The right gait is important, so that it does not over-tire or run its soles sore because of a poor gait. The dog learns to set its pace and spread its strength, so that it can keep up a speed of 8 miles per hour over a long period without tiring.

The exam requires the dog to cover a distance of 13 miles at a speed of between 7.5 and 9 miles per hour (with two pauses). This test proves whether the dog is physically fit and whether heart and lungs function properly.

Guard-dog training

This training consists of three elements: tracking, obedience and guard work (arrest work).

The guard work portion is both interesting and spectacular. However, the dog must be totally obedient before you can train it. People often think that arrest training makes a dog spiteful and untrustworthy, but the opposite is true. During guard service a dog must be extremely controlled, disciplined and easy to handle, and for this reason there are high demands in terms of obedience for guard service.

Tracker-dog training

In tracker-dog training, the dog must display secure tracking abilities and track a scent that is 1 mile long and at least three hours old. There are seven turns in the scent (matching the terrain). The trace is crossed by two distracting scents a good distance from each other. There are also seven obstacles at varying distances on the track.

Traffic-training

All Bullmastiffs that want to take part in training examinations, working trials, and competitions should be traffic-trained. This course is all about the handling of a dog in modern urban traffic.

It consists of an obedience element (walking on the lead, walking free, sitting on command, staying combined with the "come!" command) and a practical element which takes place on public roads and squares. The behaviour of the dog towards pedestrians and cyclists coming up from behind is examined, also its behaviour in difficult traffic situations. Then one tests the behaviour of a dog alone for a short time and how it behaves towards other animals. At the end the dog has to pass some obedience exercises in traffic.

Behaviour and obedience

This is a continuation of the traffic-training course, but where the traffic element is dropped and the obedience element expanded. During exams, the dog is tested for the components such as reacting to a gunshot (noise reaction), jumping over a one-metre hedge and going to, and returning to, a specific place.

The dog also has to stay quiet while being physically examined and measured. Before the examination the judge tests the dog for openness. He checks whether the dog can be approached without problems and that it doesn't show any serious behavioural faults.

If you plan to participate in dog shows with your Bullmastiff, you have to realise that such an activity can be of no more than little importance or interest for your dog.

Shows

Visiting a show is highly recommended if you want to learn more about a certain breed. You will also be able to get into direct contact with breeders and other owners.

Showing animals is a very competitive sport, in which breeders and exhibitors invest a lot of time. Some breeders even dedicate their life to this. There are many things to be considered. You need to choose which shows to enter and what you need to achieve for the dog to be awarded a title. The entry forms, payments, hotel reservations, everything needs to be taken care of well in advance. If you want to make a good appearance in the ring with your dog, you should also find appropriate clothing for yourself. Of course, most important of all is your dog itself. Showing a dog requires a lot of preparation. You cannot simply start preparing your dog a few weeks before the show, but you must start to prepare it for a show career when it is still very young, as it takes a lot of training until a dog presents itself well.

For some breeds, many dogs compete in the classes, and this will make it a lot more difficult to win a title. Sometimes, the representative of a very rare breed may be crowned Champion, without the dog ever having competed against another one of its kind. It is also possible for the judge to withhold the award. In order to become Champion your dog needs to have three Challenge Certificates awarded by three different judges. Of those three, at least one should be achieved when the dog is twelve months or older. Challenge Certificates can also be awarded to the best of each sex in a breed.

The British system allows a certain number of dogs per breed to be awarded the Challenge Certificate. The annual limit of Challenge Certificates to be awarded to representatives of a certain breed may be 30 or just 6. When the dogs enter the ring, the judge looks at them very carefully. Each dog is examined visually and by hand. The breed standards of many dog breeds contain remarks regarding the build. The teeth will also be examined, as each breed standard will have its own notes regarding an undershot jaw or scissor bite.

It is understandable that the judge will need to feel the dog in order to fully compare it to the breed standard. The breed standards also contain notes on gait and movement, which is why the judge will also need to see your dog move. Judges also pay attention to the way a dog carries its head and tail.

Ring craft classes

Here you are taught how to prepare yourself and your dog in the best possible way to take part in a show and how to present your dog when the big day has finally arrived. After this ring craft classes you should be able to show your dog in a way that it makes the best possible impression in the ring and with the judge. It is a good idea to first visit a show as a spectator, so that you get to know the procedure of a show.

There are usually several classes, e.g. one for puppies and one for more experienced dogs. The classes are usually very sociable events, where training is combined with lots of fun. It is not easy to teach a dog and his master all the tricks of showing.
Even if you do not plan to follow a showing career with your dog, it is still a good idea to take it to a course. Your dog will learn to socialize with people that he does not know and with other dogs. It will also learn to walk on the lead properly without being distracted. Some clubs which organise ring craft classes also organise friendly unofficial shows and Companion Dog Shows for their members once in a while.

Dog Clubs

There is a large number of dog clubs in the UK. For more information, look on the site of The Kennel Club, and click on the Breed Standard button.

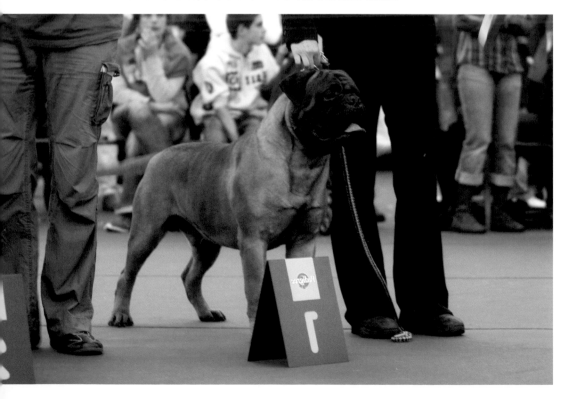

Types of Shows

There are different types of shows, of which we will give a very brief overview here.
Single Breed Shows (for one breed only, organised by a breed club)
Companion Dog Shows (for charitable causes)

Open shows (you can qualify for Crufts at some of these shows
All dog clubs organise dog shows. You must enter your dog in advance in a certain class. These meetings are usually small and friendly and are often the first acquaintance dog and master make with a "real" judge. This is an overwhelming experience for your dog - a lot of its contemporaries and a strange man or woman who fiddles around with it and peers into its mouth. After a few times, your dog will know exactly what's expected of it and will happily go to the next club match.

Championship Shows (the most prestigious shows, often the possibility to qualify for Crufts and to attain Challenge Certificates).
Various championship shows take place during the course of the year with different prizes. These shows are much more strictly organised than club-matches. Your dog must be registered in a certain class in advance and it will then be listed in a catalogue. On the day itself, the dog is usually kept on a bench until its turn comes up. During the judging in the ring, it is important that you show your dog at its best. The judge examines each dog in turn. When all the dogs from that class have been judged, the best are selected and placed. After all the judging for is finished, all the winners of the various classes in one sex compete for the

Dont forget
If you're planning to take your dog to a club match or in fact to any show, you need to be well prepared. Don't forget the following:
For yourself:
• Show documents if they have been sent to you
• Food and drink
• Clip for the catalogue number
• Chairs if an outdoor show
For your dog:
• Food and water bowls and food
• Dog blanket and perhaps a cushion
• Show lead
• Rewarding treats
• Grooming equipment
• A benching chain and collar

Challenge Certificate (3 Challenge Certificates from different judges and your Bullmastiff will be a Champion in the UK).
The best Bullmastiff in the eyes of the judge gets this award. Finally, the winners of each sex compete for the title of Best in Show.

Of course, your dog must look very smart for the show. The judge will not be impressed it its coat is not clean and its paws are dirty. Nails must be clipped and the teeth must be free of plaque. The dog must also be free from parasites and ailments. A bitch must not be in season and a male must be in possession of both testicles. Apart from those things, judges also hate badly brought-up, anxious or nervous dogs. Get in touch with your local dog club or the breed association if you want to know more about shows. Apart from those things, judges also hate badly brought up dogs, anxious or nervous dogs. Get in touch with the local dog club or the breed association if you want to know more about dog shows.

Parasites

All dogs are vulnerable to various sorts of parasites. Parasites are tiny creatures that live at the expense of another animal. They feed on blood, skin and other body substances.

There are two main types. Internal parasites live within their host animal's body (tapeworm and roundworm for example) and external parasites live on the animal's exterior, usually in its coat (fleas, lice and ticks), but also in its ears (ear mite).

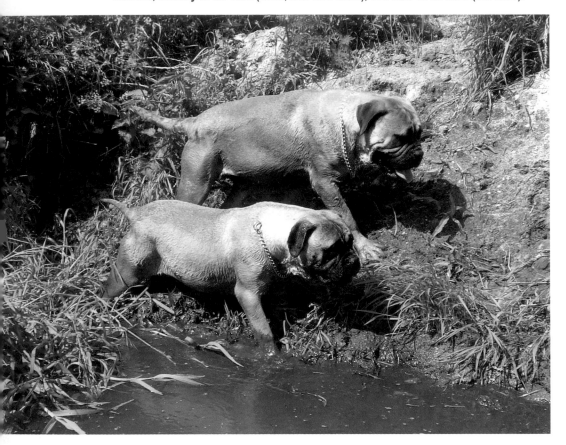

Fleas

Fleas feed on a dog's blood. They cause not only itching and skin problems, but can also carry infections such as tapeworm. In large numbers they can cause anaemia and dogs can also become allergic to a flea's saliva, which can cause serious skin conditions. So it is important to treat your dog against fleas as effectively as possible, do not just treat the dog itself but also its surroundings. For treatment of the animal, there are various medicines: drops for the neck, drops to put in its food, flea collars, long-life sprays and flea powders. There are various sprays in pet shops that can be used to eradicate fleas in the dog's immediate surroundings. Choose a spray that kills both adult fleas and their larvae. If your dog goes into your car, you should spray that too. Fleas can also affect other pets, so you should treat those too. When spraying a room, cover any aquariums or fishbowls. If the spray reaches the water, it can be fatal for your fish! Your vet and pet shop have a wide range of flea treatments and can advise you on this subject.

Ticks

Ticks are small, spider-like parasites. They feed on the blood of the animal or person they have settled on. A tick looks like a tiny, grey-coloured leather bag with eight feet. When it has sucked itself full, it can easily be five to ten times its own size and be darker in colour. Dogs usually fall victim to ticks in bushes, woods or long grass. Ticks cause not only irritation by their blood-sucking, but can also carry a number of serious diseases. This applies especially to the Mediterranean countries, where ticks can be infected with blood parasites. In our country these diseases are fortunately less common, but Lyme disease, which can also affect humans, has reached our shores as well. Your vet can prescribe a special treatment if you are planning to take your dog to southern Europe. It is important to fight ticks as effectively as possible.

Flea

Tick

Tapeworm

Check your dog regularly, especially when it has been running free in woods and bushes. Your dog can also wear an anti-tick collar.

Removing a tick is simple when using tick tweezers. Grip the tick with the tweezers, very close to the dog's skin, and carefully pull it out. You can also grip the tick between your fingers and by using a turning movement, pull it carefully out. You must disinfect the spot where the tick had been, by using iodine to prevent infection. Never soak the tick in alcohol, ether or oil. In a shock reaction the tick may discharge the infected contents of its stomach into the dog's skin and infect your dog.

Roundworm

Worms

Dogs can suffer from various types of worm. The most common ones are tapeworm and roundworm. Tapeworm causes diarrhoea and poor general condition. With a tapeworm infection you can sometimes find small pieces of the worm around the dog's anus or on its bed. In this case, the dog must be wormed. You should also check your dog for fleas, which carry the tapeworm infection. Roundworm is a condition that reoccurs regularly. Puppies always are infected through their mother's milk. Your vet has medicines to prevent roundworm. Roundworm causes problems such as diarrhoea, loss of weight and stagnated growth, particularly in younger dogs. You might find roundworms in the faeces of the dog. In serious cases the pup becomes thin, but with a swollen belly. It may vomit and you can then see the worms in its vomit. They are spaghetti-like tendrils. A puppy must be treated against worms every two weeks from its 3rd week onwards until it is three months old. When the puppy has reached the age of three months, it has to be treated every three months during its first year. Adult dogs should be treated every six months. And of course when you notice that your dog is infected by worms, you treat it more often.

Health

We now go into some medical ups and downs of the Bullmastiff. We want to give some brief information about ailments and disorders that affect this breed more than other dogs.

There is not enough room in this book to deal with all the medical ups and downs of the Bullmastiff. We will limit ourselves to dealing with some illnesses and abnormalities, which are more common with the Bullmastiff than with any other breed.

Breed-specific conditions

Breeders not only do their utmost to meet the breed standard as much as possible when breeding puppies. Also the health of their puppies is extremely important to breeders and a breeder will do everything that is possible to prevent disorders. In case a dog gets ill, it does not always say that the breeder is to blame for that. The best thing is to discuss this honestly with the breeder and a solution certainly will be found.

Here below we discuss several disorders that affect the Bullmastiff more than other breeds. However, this does not mean that your dog will get one of these disorders.

Health Issues in the Bullmastiff

Like many large breeds, Hip Dysplasia and Elbow Dysplasia are health issues that can affect the Bullmastiff. The Bullmastiff is also vulnerable for Bloat, a condition most often found in large, deep chested dog breeds. Some kidney disorders and some eye-diseases are found within this breed.

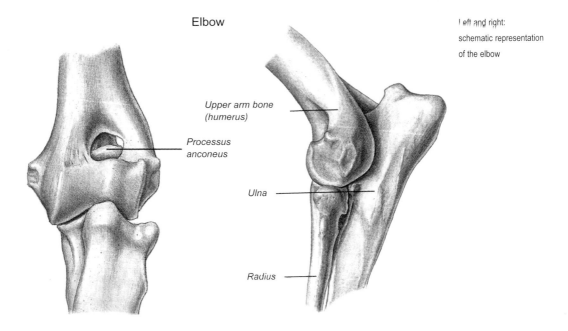

Elbow

Left and right:
schematic representation
of the elbow

Upper arm bone
(humerus)

Processus
anconeus

Ulna

Radius

Hip & Elbow Dysplasia

Canine Hip Dysplasia afflicts millions of dogs each year and can result in debilitating orthopaedic disease of the hip. It is caused when the femoral head does not fit properly in the hip socket, causing instability of the joint. Over time, this malformation can cause degenerative joint disease which causes increased pain and immobility.

Hip Dysplasia (HD)

Bullmastiffs, as many other breeds, are vulnerable to HD. Although in this country we tend not to do much about Hip Dysplasia, we should be aware of what it is. Hip Dysplasia is an abnormality of the hip joints in the hind quarters, whereby the socket of the hip joint and the head of the upper thigh do not match properly, This causes an inflammation and bone tumours, which can be very painful. Until recently, it was assumed that HD was primarily caused by genetic factors.

Recent investigations, however, indicate that while genetic factors certainly play a role in terms of a dog's susceptibility to HD, external factors such as food quality and exercise appear at least equally important. Limit the chance of HD as far as possible by giving your dog ready-made food of a good brand, and never add any supplements! Make sure your dog does not get too fat. A Bullmastiff pup should be somewhat protected from HD in its first year. Do not let it romp too much with other dogs, chase sticks and balls too wildly or run up and down stairs. These kinds of games cause the pup to make abrupt and risky movements, which can overburden its soft joints. One important but under-estimated factor behind HD is the floor in your home. Parquet and tiled floors are much too slippery for a young dog. Regular slipping can cause complications that promote HD. If you have a smooth floor, it is advisable to lay blankets or old carpets in places the dog uses regularly. Let it spend lots of time in the garden as grass is a perfect surface to run on.

The breed associations try to keep control by strictly testing potential breeding animals. An examination for HD is therefore mandatory for all animals intended for breeding. In case a breeding association does not have these strict rules it is highly advisable to have the breeding animal checked, to make sure that you breed with healthy dogs only.

Elbow Dysplasia

Elbow Dysplasia may be due to different growth rates of the three bones making up the elbow. In affected dogs, the joint is lax or loose and, in mildly affected dogs, leads to painful arthritis.

Allergies

Some Bullmastiffs react allergically to various substances. We know of contact-allergy, food-allergy, allergy for substances that are taken in by breathing. Flea-allergy is also a well known example. Allergy is shown through a reaction of the skin. These disorders can be temporary, although they can also become chronic. The time of the year can play a major role with allergies.

The hair is often gone in certain spots, because the dogs licks and bites itself, as these spots are itching. Get in touch with your veterinarian, because itching is worse than pain.

Bloat

Gastric Dilatation Volvulus (GDV) is a condition caused by a twisting of the stomach and thus trapping the stomach contents and gases, resulting in a rapid swelling of the abdomen accompanied by pain and eventual death if untreated. It is an emergency, requiring immediate veterinary action.

This condition is most often found in large, deep chested dog breeds. Anyone owning a deep chested breed, susceptible to Bloat should be prepared to handle the emergency procedures necessary, including having the name and phone number of emergency clinics and/or after-hour vets readily available.

Symptoms can be subtle. You should learn to recognize them:
- Continuous pacing and/or lying down in odd places
- Salivating, panting, whining
- Unable to get comfortable
- Acting agitated.
- Unproductive vomiting or retching (may produce frothy foamy vomit in small quantities)
- Excessive drooling, usually accompanied by retching noises
- Swelling in abdominal area (may or may not be noticeable)

If ANY combination of these symptoms is noticed, CALL YOUR VET and get the dog there as fast as possible. Bloat is LIFE-THREATENING.

Kidney diseases

Within the Bullmastiff breed, several kidney disorders have been found. Here below you find some brief details.

Cystinuria

Cystinuria is an inborn error of the amino acid transport that results in the defective absorption by the kidneys of the amino acid called cystine. The name means "cystine in the urine." Cystinuria is an inborn error of amino acid transport that results in the defective absorption by the kidneys of the amino acid called cystine.

Cystinuria is a genetic disorder that currently cannot be prevented. Cystinuria is a recessive gene.

More information on cystinuria you can find at www.cystinuria.com

Glomerulonephritis

Acute glomerulonephritis is an inflammatory disease of both kidneys. Acute glomerulonephritis most often follows a streptococcal infection of the throat or skin. Chronic glomerulonephritis can develop over a period of several years and very often it will be noticed in a late stage. Acute glomerulonephritis is an inflammation of the glomeruli, bundles of tiny vessels inside the kidneys. The damaged glomeruli cannot effectively filter waste products and excess water from the bloodstream to make urine. The kidneys appear enlarged, fatty, and congested. A kidney biopsy may also be performed, using ultrasound to guide the needle to obtain the specimen.

Renal amyloidosis

Amyloidosis is a progressive, incurable, metabolic disease characterized by abnormal deposits of protein in one or more organs or body systems. Amyloid proteins are manufactured by malfunctioning bone marrow. Amyloidosis, which occurs when accumulated amyloid deposits impair normal body function, can cause organ failure or death. It is assumed that renal amyloidosis is not a hereditary disorder in Bullmastiffs.

Juvenile renal disease

Juvenile Renal Disease is the last one in the overview. When a dog is suffering from Juvenile Renal Disease, the kidneys do not develop during its growth. The disease is often first recognized when puppies cannot be house-trained. Vomiting, loss of weight and a strong breath are also some of the symptoms.

Cross-sectional view
of the eye

Labels: Ciliary body, Iris, Cornea, Lens, Aqueous humor, Retina, Optic nerve, Blind spot, Vitreous

Eye diseases

Entropion

Entropion occurs regularly with the Bullmastiff. Entropion is a condition where the eyelid curls to the inside, so that the hairs from the coat irritate the eyeball. The dog blinks a lot and the eyes water constantly. Surgical correction is necessary with this condition. Dogs that are affected by this eye disease can never be used for breeding, even not after surgery.

Entropion

Progressive Retina Atrophy (PRA)

Progressive Retina Atrophy is an awful condition. Once it has found its way into a bloodline, PRA is difficult to eradicate. The disease is a progressive degeneration of the retina that inevitably leads to blindness. In the early stages, the dog will still be able to see well in daylight until it is about five years old, but between its fifth and ninth year, the dog will become totally blind.

PRA

Diseases caused by viruses and other organisms

Pseudo rabies

Pseudo rabies or Aujeszky's disease is actually a disease found in pigs. The virus is transferred to other animals when they eat raw pork which is infected. The disease affects the central nervous system. A dog which has been infected with the virus becomes restless, apathetic, nervous and loses its appetite. Aujeszky's disease progresses incredibly quickly: the animal will become paralysed and die within a week. There is no cure. Therefore never feed dogs (or other pets) raw or not properly cooked pork.

Corona

Corona is a viral disease, the symptoms of which are vomiting and diarrhoea.
This disease looks like a parvo virus infection, but is less severe in its progress. Besides the symptoms listed under parvo virus, other symptoms include damage to the mucous membranes, which manifests itself in eye and nose discharge. The disease is spread via faeces.

Hepatitis

Hepatitis is a highly infectious liver disease. The virus is found in both dogs and foxes. The noticeable symptoms vary widely. Approximately one week after infection, the body temperature increases, after which the animal's temperature starts to fluctuate.
The dog remains lively during the first few days, but this changes. Symptoms include: coughing and an inflamed throat, moist eyes, lack of appetite, sometimes in combination with vomiting and/or diarrhoea. The dog's eyes will cloud over. The virus is spread via the urine of infected dogs. As infected dogs urinate in parks and against trees, the disease spreads very quickly.
Hepatitis symptoms vary from light fever to a very serious liver infection. If the disease is treated at an early stage, there is a chance of full recovery. If the liver is infected, the fever will run very high and the dog will no longer eat. Invariably, if the disease reaches this stage the dog will die. Hepatitis can cause young dogs and puppies to die very suddenly.

Hepatitis is not always easy to diagnose, as the symptoms are very similar to those of Carré's disease.

Carré's disease

This disease is caused by a virus and is highly infectious. The severity of the first symptoms, a runny nose and some coughing, is often underestimated. Shortly after that, fever, lack of appetite, vomiting and/or diarrhoea follow. Furthermore, the dog will suffer from an inflamed throat and pussy discharge from the nose and eyes, spasms and cramps. A young dog may suddenly become severely ill. The virus causes inflammation in the intestines, but also meningitis. Many dogs do not survive this disease. The dogs that do survive, often suffer permanent nerve damage, or a 'tick'. Many dogs have behavioural disorders which they did not have before the infection, e.g. orientation problems. The disease is spread via saliva, urine and faeces.

Rabies

This viral disease is fatal to humans and dogs. The virus enters the body when saliva from an infected animal reaches a wound of a hitherto healthy animal. It spreads via nerves to the brain, and will eventually kill the animal. After being bitten by an infected animal, it can take up to 50 days before the new victim shows any symptoms. The final phase of this disease is terrible.

The brain is affected by the virus, the dog is terrified, hides in a corner, and its behaviour can suddenly switch, i.e. the sweetest dog may suddenly become feral and very aggressive. It will bite everything and attack anything that comes close to it. Luckily, rabies does not exist in the UK, but if you are planning to take your dog abroad, you should have it vaccinated against rabies. Rabies is spread via the saliva (bites) of foxes, badgers and other animals.

Kennel cough

The kennel cough syndrome is caused by a number of different micro-organisms: Para-influenza virus, Bordetella and others.

The disease usually spreads where many dogs are kept closely together, such as in a kennel, dog hotel, at a show or at dog schools. The symptoms of this respiratory problem are a harsh, rough cough and occasionally damage to the lungs.

Dogs do not usually become severely ill from kennel cough, but you must have your dog treated by a vet. Cough medicine (thyme syrup) can help to soften the mucous membranes and a holiday to a place with lots of fresh air can do wonders. If you are going to leave your dog in a boarding kennel, it is best (and usually also required) to have your dog vaccinated against kennel cough. You should have your dog vaccinated against this obnoxious cough approximately four weeks before it goes to kennels. The disease is spread via the breath.

Parvo virus

Parvo virus is a highly infectious viral disease. A dog infected with the parvo virus will usually not survive. The virus is spread via the faeces of an infected dog.

When a healthy dogs sniffs at these faeces, it becomes infected straight away. The virus penetrates to the intestines, where it causes serious inflammation. Within a very short time, the dog will suffer bloody diarrhoea, may vomit blood, become drowsy, develop a fever and become very seriously ill.

The dog will usually also not eat or drink and can therefore dehydrate. Treatment primarily consists of administering large amounts of fluid intravenously. Most dogs die within 48 hours after the first symptoms. In puppies, an infection with parvo virus can cause cardiac arrest. Nowadays, puppies are usually vaccinated against parvo virus very early in life. Puppies which have survived the disease may unfortunately die very suddenly later on due to angina.

Weil's disease

Weil's disease (leptospirosis) is a disease caused by micro-organisms. Dogs are most commonly infected in spring or autumn. In younger dogs, the disease can easily be fatal. Humans can also be infected through dogs or rats. A dog swimming in contaminated water might contract bacteria via the mucous membranes or tiny wounds on the skin. The bacteria gather in the liver and kidneys. The symptoms include: high fever, drowsiness and muscle pain. Furthermore, the dog suffers from a lack of appetite, vomiting and is very thirsty.

The dog may also suffer from nose bleeds, dark urine and sometimes yellow fever. The disease is spread via the urine of infected rats and dogs.

First aid for dogs

When your dog gets injured or ill, the time that passes before professional medical help is available can be crucial. Whatever you do or do not do in this time can save your pet's life.

Bear in mind that the first aid you apply is only intended to gain control over acute emergency situations. Your dog may have suffered internal injuries, which you cannot see. Therefore always take your dog to a veterinarian for examination!

If you are in any doubt about anything, ask your vet for advice. He will certainly understand if you are uncertain about what to do. Applying medical aid to an animal always has one complication: communication with the patient. You cannot explain to a dog that you are trying to help it and lessen its pain. A seriously injured animal is scared and in a lot of pain. It will therefore often try to escape or to attack its helper(s). You must therefore restrain the dog so that you do not get hurt. At the same time, you must make it clear to the animal, through a firm but friendly approach, that you are in control of the situation, but still sympathetic. Keep on talking calmly and frequently address the animal by its name. The tone of your voice and hearing its name will have a calming, relaxing effect. Lay or sit the dog on a table. This makes it more difficult for the animal to escape and it makes treatment easier for you.

Not all cases requiring first aid are the same. One situation may be more severe than another and may require quicker intervention. There is a fixed order of treatment, from very severe to less severe.

It is therefore very important to stick to this order when treating wounds and conditions: a beautiful support bandage will not do any good if the victim died in the meantime because it could not breathe anymore. In the overview on the next page you will see which life functions must be restored first, before you begin with treating the next function.

Order of treatment
1.   Respiration
2.   Heart function
3.   Blood vessels
4.   Shock
5.   Poisoning
6.   Fractures
7   Digestive tract
8.   Other injuries

1. Respiration

Together with the heart function, breathing is an animal's most important vital function. By breathing, oxygen is absorbed into the body, which is necessary to allow the organs and tissues to function properly. If an oxygen deficit goes on for too long, the organs and tissues will become damaged very quickly and eventually die off. If respiration stops, the animal is in acute danger. A dog with breathing difficulties often stretches its neck and tries to inhale air with all its might. The mucous membranes of the tongue and the eyes turn blue and the animal will become unconscious after a while. If your dog is lying absolutely still and you cannot see anything on first sight, check the breathing by laying your hand or a few fingers on the chest: you should feel it moving up and down.

If your dog is suffering from breathing difficulties, take it to fresh air immediately. Try to get behind the cause of the breathing difficulties as quickly as possible and eliminate it as soon as you can. Remove any possibly obstructing objects from the neck (collars, flea collars). Check that no objects are stuck in the throat or windpipe. Do not be too careful, as every second counts now! In some cases you can apply a short thrust on the chest and push the object out with the air from the lungs. Applying pressure on the outside of the throat will also sometimes help.

If the dog is choking on water, you need to lift it up by its back legs with the head hanging down. This allows the fluid to drain from the lungs. Then push on the chest a few times to remove the last remaining fluid from the lungs.

If the breathing still does not pick up, you will need to apply mouth-to-mouth resuscitation to your dog. Try to take the victim to the veterinatian as quickly as possible, continuing to apply mouth-to-mouth resuscitation during the journey.

Possible causes of respiratory problems:
- Too little oxygen in the environment (insufficient ventilation, plastic bag, box);
- Water, gas or smoke in the lungs (drowning, carbon monoxide, fire);
- Swallowed objects, swelling of the mucous membranes in the respiratory tract (asthmatic attack, inflammation), swelling of the tongue (wasp's sting);
- Restricted throat (collar, flea collar);
- Damage to the diaphragm, broken ribs;
- Damaged lungs;
- Choking on food (through fright) or vomit.

Loss of consciousness
A dog can lose its consciousness for a number of reasons. Epilepsy, a heavy blow, brain haemorrhaging and poisoning are some possibilities. Loss of consciousness is always an emergency, in which case you need to act as follows:
- Get someone to notify the vet straight away;
- Lay the dog on its side, as long as you cannot detect a wound there, with the paws pointing away from the body. The head needs to lay somewhat higher than the rest of the body;
- Check the pulse. If necessary, apply heart massage.
- Check the respiration. If necessary, apply mouth-to-mouth resuscitation;
- When the dog is breathing (again), pull its tongue out of its mouth and remove any food remains;
- Do not give the victim food or water;
- Keep the animal warm with a blanket.

2. Heart function

A dog can also suffer a heart attack. Not every heart attack results in cardiac arrest.
Some causes of heart attacks include drowning, suffocation, poisoning, severe allergic reaction, trauma or electric shock.
Symptoms include pain, shortness of breath, nausea or vomiting and dizziness.
Do not think that it will pass over. If you suspect heart failure, you must take your dog to the veterinarian as quickly as possible.

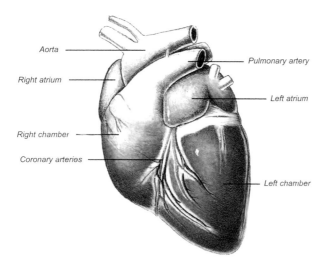

Above: schematic representation of the heart

Below: cross-sectional view of the heart

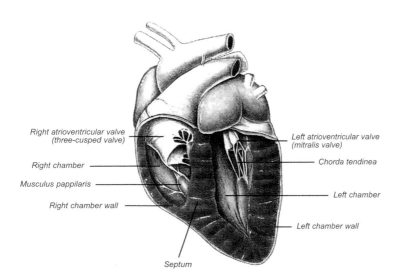

3. Blood vessels
Bleeding
A dog can become injured and lose blood. In the case of serious blood loss, the animal may die. How much blood is lost and how quickly depends on the size of the wound, but also on the type of blood vessel. We differentiate between three types of bleeding, depending on the type of blood vessel injured:

Capillary bleeding
This is a fairly harmless bleeding; however, it does need to be treated. The wound is not deep (often only a scrape) and there is little loss of blood. Disinfect the wound well. Briefly press it closed with some gauze. You often do not even need to dress it.

Venous bleeding
In this type of bleeding the blood streams out of the wound steadily and is dark red in colour. This is because the blood is flowing towards the heart through the veins and is low in oxygen. Clean the wound well with a disinfectant tissue or sterile gauze soaked in boiled water and then dress it. Take your dog to the veterinarian straight away. He will again disinfect the wound thoroughly and stitch it if necessary.

Arterial bleeding

This is a very serious type of bleeding, which can be fatal for your dog. The blood gushes out of the wound intermittently and is light red in colour. This is because it comes straight from the heart and contains a lot of oxygen. The victim loses a lot of blood in a very short time. You therefore need to act very quickly:

- Hold the dog with a restraining grip and try to calm it. Use your voice to prevent it losing consciousness.
- First check respiration and pulse, and try to stop the bleeding after that.
- Lay the bleeding part of the body higher than the rest of the body
- Put some sterile gauze or a clean cloth on the wound, and exert pressure with the palm of your hand, so that the blood vessel is squeezed tight. If necessary, put some extra gauze or cotton wool on the wound and exert more pressure. On spots where the skin is loose (lips, cheeks, scruff), tightly push the wound edges together in your fist.
- When the bleeding has stopped, put a thick layer of cotton wool on the gauze or cloth. Bandage the wound with a tight bandage. Keep on exerting pressure.
- Take the animal to the veterinarian as quickly as possible.

Major bleeding at the foot or tail can be stopped by exerting pressure on one of the so-called pressure points with your finger. These are points where the blood vessels run closely under the skin and are easily squeezed tight.

If you cannot manage to stop arterial bleeding in the manner described above, you can apply a tourniquet as a last resort. A tourniquet must never be applied around the neck or head! After applying a tourniquet, take the victim to the veterinarian as quickly as possible. Be aware that a dog can go into shock as a result of serious bleeding.

Minor cut and stab wounds:

- Hold the victim in a restraining grip. It will probably try to resist.
- Wash your hands thoroughly and use sterile material from a first aid kit as much as possible.
- Remove any hairs that might be in the wound: dampen them with clean water, stroke them out of the wound and cut them off close to the skin. Examine the depth of the wound.
- Rinse the wound clean with a mild disinfectant, which is dissolved in water. You can also dissolve two teaspoons of salt in a litre of tap water. Try to gently rub open small deep stab wounds.
- Wash the skin around the wound with disinfectant shampoo. Cover the wound with sterile gauze, to prevent suds getting in. Rinse with plenty of clean water afterwards.

- With graze wounds, in particular, there may be (a lot of) dirt in the skin. Remove it with a cotton bud or a corner of a clean cloth. Be very careful when doing this!
- Dab the wound dry with a clean, non-fluffy cloth.
- Put disinfectant salve on the wound and bandage it.
- Change the dressing every day and pay close attention to possible wound infections.
- If a scab has formed, you need to prevent the animal removing it. Keep the wound edges supple with Vaseline or cod-liver oil salve.

Major cuts or skin parts missing:

- In these cases your first aid attempts must be directed towards getting the animal to the veterinarian as quickly as possible, and to prevent the situation from worsening.
- The dog might be in a lot of pain. If necessary, apply a restraining grip.
- Remove any big objects, such as splinters, stones and twigs, from the wound. Do not remove objects that have penetrated deeply into the skin. If they stick far out of the wound, cut them off above the skin.
- Soak a clean cloth in a solution of two teaspoons of salt in one litre of water. Lay the wet cloth on the wound and fixate it with tape or bandage clamps.
- Keep the cloth wet with the saline solution during the transport to the veterinarian.
- Make sure that the animal cannot lick or bite at the wound.
- A big cut needs to be stitched by a vet within six hours. This will speed up the healing process.

A dog can also encounter wounds when the skin is still intact. Examples of this are bruises or haemorrhages. You can treat these by applying ice cubes which are wrapped in a tea towel. Your dog can also suffer more serious, internal damage. Symptoms include lightening of the mucous membranes and/or bloody discharge of slime from the nose. In the case of internal injuries, you must not move your dog or let it drink: call a vet straight away!

Burns

The skin is a very important organ for any animal. It protects the body against damaging external influences by giving it the right signals (e.g. it is warm, something is pinching). The skin also sends signals from the animal to its surroundings, e.g. hairs standing up. The coat is covered with aromatic substances, sweat and fats which come from the skin. Finally the skin also regulates the body's temperature and the dog's water balance: it makes sure that the body does not dehydrate in a warm environment. Burns can have serious consequences, especially when major parts of the skin have been affected. In these cases the skin can no longer fulfil its vital functions.

In the case of burns you always need to apply first aid. The animal will be in a lot of pain and will need to be examined by a vet as soon as possible. He will judge if the animal can be saved. Whether an animal can recover depends on the percentage of skin damaged and on how deeply the damage penetrates the skin.

In the case of burns you can try to prevent the condition worsening by thoroughly cooling off the animal as quickly as possible. Proceed as follows:

- Cool the burnt part of the skin with cold water as soon as possible (if necessary by dumping the victim in a pond or bucket). The cold not only alleviates the pain, but also gets the warmth out of the skin, which prevents deeper skin layers being seriously damaged.
- You need to cool off the dog for at least ten minutes. Carefully dab dry the area around the affected spot, but do not touch the wound: the risk of infection is too great.
- Do not put any salve or grease on the wound.
- Cover the wound with a clean cloth soaked in a solution of two teaspoons of salt in a litre of water. Keep the cloth damp with this solution during your drive to the veterinarian.
- Give the dog small amounts of water - if it can still swallow - over small time intervals (the mucous membranes of the throat and mouth may have been affected by the smoke).
- Burnt skin can no longer contain body warmth, which means that the dog may shake because of the cold. Keep it warm with a blanket.
- Even if your dog is obviously in a lot of pain: never feed it painkillers or sedatives of your own accord.

Bite wounds

It can happen that your dog gets bitten by a feral animal, such as a fox or a stray cat or dog. First of all, you should clean the wound with disinfectant. Take your dog to the veterinarian as quickly as possible for further treatment!

4. Shock

Shock is not actually a condition as such, but can be the result of serious injuries combined with severe blood loss, a bad fright and pain. An injured animal may also become stressed by your attempts to treat it, which can also easily lead to shock. Preventing shock is actually more important than treating it. In the case of shock, too little blood is pumped through the body. If this carries on for long, tissues and organs do not receive enough oxygen. This means that they can die off. If the brain gets insufficient oxygen, the animal will lose consciousness.

In cases where there is a real chance of the dog going into shock, you need to act as follows: Free the respiratory tract by drawing the tongue a little out of the mouth. Check first if there are any objects in the throat or mouth. If necessary, apply mouth-to-mouth resuscitation and/or heart massage and stop any bleeding. An animal with very high fever or heatstroke (sunstroke) needs to be cooled with cold, wet cloths applied to the head and neck. Bring the animal into quiet, dark surroundings. Make sure that the head is positioned a little higher than the rest of the body. In case of shock keep the animal warm with a blanket and maybe with a hot water bottle (maximum 45°C). Alternatively, in the case of sunstroke keep it cool.

If the animal can still drink, give it small amounts of water. Never offer it anything to drink if there is any suspicion of internal damage! Take the animal to the veterinarian as quickly as possible. He will put it on a drip to stabilise the blood pressure.

Causes of shock:
- Cardiac arrest
- Severe bleeding
- Dehydration
- Bad fright
- Severe pain
- Poisoning
- Allergies
- Brain trauma
- Serious burns
- Severe stress
- Malignant tumours
- Septicaemia
- Sunstroke
- High fever
- Prolonged vomiting/ diarrhoea

Speedy actions can prevent the animal actually going into shock! If you see the following symptoms, you need to apply first aid immediately:
- Weak, irregular pulse
- Hectic, superficial breathing
- Cold ears and feet
- Pale skin (abdomen and inner thighs) and pale mucous membranes (mouth, eyes) and ears
- Apathy and anxiety

Epileptic seizure

A seizure can be very brief or rather long. The dog will fall over and stay lying in an abnormal position with convulsions. It may urinate, drool or have widened pupils.

After a seizure your dog will be exhausted and gasping from the exertion. The animal is dull and uncoordinated. An epileptic fit looks very serious and can cause panic in anyone witnessing it. With properly applied first aid, the whole situation is a lot less serious than it looks. Therefore stay calm and proceed as follows:

- Carefully drag the dog by its back legs or body to a place where it cannot injure itself through its thrashing movements. For example, never leave it lying at the top of the stairs.
- Try to lessen the convulsions somewhat by putting a blanket or cloth over the animal and by surrounding it with cushions. This also decreases the risk of the animal injuring itself.
- Never try to apply a halter or hold the animal in a restraining grip. Also do not give your dog any food, water or medication. (valium/diazepam suppositories)
- If necessary, apply mouth-to-mouth resuscitation. Watch your fingers when the dog starts breathing on its own again.
- Let the dog come round in a calm, dark environment. Stay and observe it for at least half an hour.
- If the seizures come back within a short interval, you are facing an emergency situation. Take the animal to the veterinarian as soon as possible.

Sunstroke

A dog may also be affected by heat. This often happens when the animal is left in a car for a long time, which is badly ventilated and standing in the sun. Sunstroke (or heatstroke) can be recognised by the following symptoms: fast, jerky breathing, a glazed look and a body temperature of more than 40°C.

Take the animal to a shady, cool place. Immerse it in a bucket or tub of cold water or hose it down. Especially sparsely haired parts of the body, such as the belly, the elbows and the groin, need to be cooled off quickly. Stop with this when the body temperature drops below 39°C. When the animal comes to, you need to dry it off and let it drink small amounts of water in intervals of a few minutes. Take the victim to the veterinarian as soon as possible.

5. Poisoning

If an animal has been poisoned, a number of different symptoms might appear. It will often have breathing problems, it will feel cold to touch and it might lose consciousness. However, it might also be shaking and hyperactive. Always bear in mind that there is an increased chance of the animal going into shock.

Take the poison away from the dog as quickly as possible, but make sure that it does not become scared. Under no circumstances must the dog be frightened and run away. Remove any remnants of the poison from its mouth or the skin with a cloth as quickly as possible. Try to find out what the poison is. Take the package or whatever is left of the toxin to the veterinarian. This might be vital when it comes to determining the right antidote. How your dog has to be treated further depends on the type of poison it has ingested.

If your dog has ingested something from the group of 'non-caustic' substances (see table), you need to make it vomit as quickly as possible. You can stimulate vomiting by placing a teaspoon of salt on the back of its tongue. Pick up some of the sick with a plastic bag and take it to the veterinarian. If the dog is unconscious, lay its head lower than the rest of the body. This allows the vomit to flow out of its mouth and prevents it from flowing into the lungs. If necessary, apply mouth-to-mouth resuscitation. If the animal cannot be taken to a vet immediately, it is best to wrap it in a blanket and to take it to a dark, quiet place. Sometimes you can read on packages of toxins which substances need to be administered as antidotes. If the dog has thrown up properly, you can give it a mix of milk and Norit. This is advisable if it will take some time before you can take your dog to the veterinarian.

Non-caustic substances:	Caustic substances:
• Anti-freeze	• Base
• Bleach (chlorine)	- Caustic soda
• Carbamates	- Many paint or wallpaper strippers
• Pesticides:	• Petrol
- Strychnine	• Petroleum
- Crimidine	• Paint thinner
• Lead (paint and roof covering)	• Acids
• Insecticides:	- Battery acid
- Parathion	- Hydrochloric acid
- Dichlorvos	
• Snail poison	

If your pet has ingested a 'caustic' substance (see table), it must not throw up under any circumstances! The mucous membranes of the mouth, throat and gullet have already been seriously damaged by the caustic toxin. If the toxin passes through them again, the damage will be more serious. Try to dilute the toxins in the digestive tract. In the case of a base toxin, give your dog vinegar or lemon juice. If you dog has ingested an acid, feed it soda or milk.

6. Fractures

Unfortunately, dogs quite regularly have broken bones or fractures. The prominent cause of fractures is road traffic accidents, but a fall from great height, a bite by another animal or a gun shot wound may also lead to fractures. When applying first aid to fractures you need to be very careful, as the hard, sharp edges of the broken bone can easily damage tissues and organs.

We differentiate two types of fractures. In closed fractures the skin has not been damaged and the fractured parts are therefore not exposed to the air. In open fractures the fractured parts break out of the skin through the wound. This type of fracture can have serious consequences, as the very sensitive bone marrow can become infected by bacteria. Such an infection can make an animal seriously ill and will slow down the healing process of the fracture.

An open fracture is obviously easy to diagnose. In the case of a closed fracture this is a little more difficult. There are, however, some symptoms which indicate a fracture: pain, swelling, loss of function in the broken limb, abnormal position of the bone, abnormal mobility of the broken limb and a grating sound during movement. When you have clearly diagnosed a fracture, you should proceed as follows:

- Hold your dog in a restraining grip and let it calm down as much as possible at the scene of the accident.
- Be aware of shock symptoms. They may occur if your dog is in a lot of pain.
- Make sure that the broken leg lies on top.
- Do not pull on the leg and make sure that the fracture is as still as possible.
- If the lower part of the leg is broken and if you need to transport the animal quite a distance, apply a preliminary splint. This can be a straight piece of wood, a piece of carton or a rolled-up newspaper. Carefully apply cotton wool or a thick cloth around the leg. Then apply the splints at the sides of the leg, so that the joints above and under the fracture can no longer move.

- Fasten the splints with tape or bandages, but do not pull them too tight. It is only a matter of immobilising the fracture for the time of transport, so that it does not move.
- Carefully push a blanket or board under the dog and lift the animal up. Make sure that it lies as quietly as possible.
- Take the animal to the veterinarian straight away.

In the case of an open fracture you need to make sure that the animal does not lick or scratch at the fracture. Put plenty of sterile gauze or a clean cloth onto the wound, so that no dirt can get into it. Do not put any salve or iodine onto it, as this only increases the risk of infection. The vet will need to treat an open fracture further.

7. Digestive tract

Vomiting

It is quite normal that dogs sometimes eat grass and throw up. They do this when their stomach bothers them. Eating grass stimulates vomiting, which means that the dog discards its stomach contents.

If a dog throws up too often, something is definitely wrong. Throwing up can have different causes, such as infections, worms, eating too much, poisoning and metabolic disturbances. Take your dog to the veterinarian as quickly as possible if it is throwing up heavily, throwing up blood and if it has a swollen belly and has a very ill appearance.

If your dog throws up regularly, but does not appear sick otherwise, you can try out whether the symptoms disappear if you feed it easily digestible food and make an appointment with your vet. You sometimes need to feed your dog before bedtime to prevent so-called 'bile vomiting' in the morning. You can buy special, easily digestible food at your pet shop or veterinarian for such cases. Divide the food into several portions per day, for example every two to four hours. Then the stomach gets the ideal opportunity to digest the food. Also make sure that your dog has plenty of fresh drinking water available. When the throwing up has stopped completely, you can carefully switch back to normal feeding. Start by replacing ten percent of the diet food with normal food. The next day you replace twenty percent, and so forth until the diet is once again one hundred percent normal food. If the problems have not disappeared, you need to contact a vet.

Diarrhoea

When your dog's faeces are soft or watery, it is suffering from diarrhoea. This is a symptom of disturbed digestion. This can have several causes, such as infection, worms, eating bad or cold food or a sudden change in the diet. If the diarrhoea is bloody, or if it is combined with symptoms such as fever, vomiting and apathy, take your dog to the veterinarian as soon as possible.

If your dog is suffering from light diarrhoea without being ill in any other way, feed it an easily digestible diet to solve the problem. Your vet or pet shop will have special, easily digestible feeds. Divide the feed into several smaller portions per day and feed it until the symptoms disappear, then slowly go back to normal food. This is best done by replacing ten percent of the diet food by normal food on the first day. On the second day you replace twenty percent and so on until the dog's diet consists of only normal food again. Always contact your vet if the diarrhoea does not stop; do not wait too long!

8. Other injuries

Bruises

To control the swelling, you can cover a bruise with a towel soaked in cold water or with ice cubes wrapped in a towel.

Traffic Accident Trauma

If you see a dog being hit by a car, do not run to it heedlessly. The last thing anyone needs in such a situation is another traffic victim! Immediately contact a vet or a pet ambulance. Make sure that other drivers become aware of the victim by clearly marking the scene of the accident. If necessary, take the victim in a restraining grip, carefully check if there are any bleeding wounds and treat the victim for shock. Carefully cover the dog with a coat or blanket. Let it lay quietly until professional help arrives. It is very important that you do not move the victim, even if no blood and wounds are visible at first sight, as the dog may have suffered internal injuries. You must also therefore not give the dog anything to drink until it has been examined by a vet.

Footpad injury

If your dog is walking awkwardly or licking its paw, there might be a splinter or another object stuck in the sole of its foot. You can carefully remove this with tweezers. Disinfect the spot with iodine straight away and bandage it. This prevents the dog licking at the wound and thus infecting it. In the case of heavy blood loss, or if the object is stuck deep in the sole, you need to take your dog to the veterinarian.

Choking

Dogs like to play with all sorts of things. It can therefore happen that the animal swallows something by accident. This can be a number of different objects, with different consequences ranging from serious to less acute. In the worst case, the swallowed object is stuck just before the windpipe. The animal can no longer breathe and this is obviously a life-threatening situation. An object which ends up in the gullet causes discomfort and sometimes a lot of pain, but the dog will not die of it immediately. You can recognise that an object is stuck in the gullet by the dog swallowing frequently and trying to throw up. The dog will drool a lot and rub its snout. In this case, proceed as follows:

- Hold your dog in a restraining grip if it does not want to accept your help.
- The dog will usually vomit; giving it food or water will only make things worse.
- An object in the gullet is a nuisance, but not life-threatening. Therefore remain calm. If the object is close to the windpipe, the animal will be in danger, which means that you need to act quickly.
- Open its mouth as far as possible and look into its throat. If the sharp teeth make it difficult to hold the snout open, take a dry tissue to carefully pull out the tongue. The dog will keep its snout open, as it will not risk biting its tongue.
- If the object is clearly visible, you can carefully remove it with tweezers or small pliers. If an object is located just before the windpipe, you can sometimes remove it by putting a finger behind it, deep in the throat. Someone else will have to push on the right spot of the throat from the outside.
- If you do not succeed, lay the dog on its side on a hard surface.
- Apply pressure just behind the last ribs, where the thorax is widest. Push downwards and forwards with both hands. This sometimes makes the object shoot out of the throat.

- Repeat this action several times quiokly one after another if you do not succeed the first time. If the object is still stuck in the throat, try removing the object from the throat with your fingers, while someone else continues pressing behind the ribs. If necessary, apply mouth-to-mouth resuscitation.
- If the object has not been removed within a few minutes, take your dog to the veterinarian as quickly as possible. Even if you did manage to remove the object, your vet will still need to examine your dog for possible complications, such as damage to the throat or gullet. Do not take any risks opening the dog's mouth or removing an object, watch your hands and fingers!

Your dog may have swallowed a sharp object, such as a splinter or a fish bone. They will usually get caught in the mucous membranes of the mouth. In this case your dog will rub its snout a lot with its paw. It will also salivate excessively, sometimes mixed with blood or retch. Some dogs might sit quietly in one corner, whereas others will run around the house like maniacs.

- Try to have a good look into your dog's throat. If necessary, apply a restraining grip.
- If you have localised the sharp object, you can carefully try to remove it. If it is stuck very tightly, leave it in the snout.
- Carefully wipe the froth from the oral cavity and take your dog to the veterinarian as quickly as possible.
- During your journey, hold onto your dog's paws, so that it cannot injure itself by continuously rubbing against its snout.
- Your vet will remove the object, probably under anaesthetic. After this, your dog will have some problems eating and will need to be fed an adjusted diet.

Wounds

A dog can become wounded in a number of ways. You may therefore encounter a wide range of wounds, which vary in their severity. Roughly, you can divide them into simple wounds, in which only the skin surface has been damaged and complex wounds, in which deeper layers, such as muscles, blood vessels and nerves have also been affected. Both types obviously need to be treated in their own way.

Always take your dog to the veterinarian if it has suffered a severe wound. Graze wounds are best cleaned with warm boiled water.

More danger

Our modern houses actually are a very strange environment for animals. There are no trees, no grass, and no shrubs. The wind does not blow around their ears. There is no stream with fresh water and no trees to scratch on. An animal needs to adapt. This does not always go smoothly, but we can make sure that its life with us is as safe as possible.

Plants

It is common knowledge that cats sometimes like to eat grass. Dogs do this too. You never know what a dog sees in a plant. Puppies in particular occassionally like to 'take a bite'. The likelihood is not big, but if it does happen, take your dog and a branch of the plant in question to your vet. He will know the best course of action. We will provide a short overview of toxic plants.

TOXIC PLANTS

-A-

Abrus precatorius	- Precatory-pea
Acer rubrum	- Red maple
Aconitum napellus	- Monk's hood
Aesculus hippocastanum	- Horse chestnut
Ailanthus altissima	- Tree-of-heaven
Allamanda cathartica	- Golden-trumper
Allium cepa	- Onion
Allium sativum	- Garlic
Alstroemeria ligtu	- Peruvian lily
Amaranthus hybridus	- Smooth pigweed
Amaryllis vittata	- Amaryllis (A. vittata)
Anthurium andraenum	- Flamingo lily
Aquilegia alpina	- Aquilegia
Asimina triloba	- Pawpaw

Aquilegia

-B-

Baptista tinctoria	- Wild indigo
Barbarea vulgaris	- Yellow rocket
Buxus sempervirens	- Buxus

Buxus

-C-

Caladium bicolor	- Caladium
Chrysanthemum indicum	- Chrysanthemum
Cicuta virosa	- Northern water-hemlock
Clematis	- Clematis
Clivia miniata	- Kaffir lily
Codiaeum variegetum	- Croton
Colchicum autumnale	- Autumn crocus
Conium macaltum	- Poison-hemlock
Convallaria majalis	- Lily-of-the-valley
Corydalis	- Corydalis
Crocus	- Crocus
Cyclamen persicum	- Cyclamen

Clematis

-D-

Dature innoxia	- Angel's trumpet
Datura stramonium	- Jimsomweed
Delphinium	- Larkspur
Dieffenbachia seguine	- Mother-in-law-plant
Digitalis purpurea	- Foxglove

Corydalis

-E-

Euonymus europaeus	- European spindletree
Euphorbia helioscopia	- Sun spurge
Euphorbia lacteal	- Candelabra-cactus
Euphorbia pulcherrima	- Poinsettia

Crocus

-F-

Fagopyrum esculentem	- Tall manna grass

-G-

| *Gutierrezia sarothrae* | - Broom snakewood |
| *Gymnocladus dioicus* | - Kentucky coffeetree |

-H-

Hedera helix	- English ivy
Helenium autumnale	- Sneezeweed
Helianthus annuus	- Sunflower
Heliotropium curassavicum	- Spatulate-leaved heliotrope
Heracleum mantegazzianum	- Giant hogweed
Humulus lupulus	- Common hop
Hyancinthoides nonscripta	- English bluebell
Hydrangea macrophylla	- Hydrangea
Hypercum perforatum	- St. John's wort

-I-

Ilex aquifolium	- English holly
Ipomoea tricolour	- Morning glory
Iris pseudocorus	- Yellow iris
Iris versicolor	- Blue flag iris

-J-

| *Juglans nigra* | - Black walnut |

-K-

| *Kalanchoe daigremontiana* | - Devil's-backbone |
| *Kalmia angustofolia* | - Sheep-laurel |

-L-

Laportea canadensus	- Canada nettle
Lathyrus odoratus	- Sweet pea
Lathyrus sativus	- Grass pea
Leonurus cardiaca	- Motherwort
Ligistrum vulgare	- Common privet
Linaria vulgaris	- Yellow toadflax
Lobelia cardinalis	- Cardinalflower
Lobelia inflate	- Indian-tobacco
Lonicera xylosteum	- Fly honeysuckle
Lupinus argenteus	- Silvery lupine
Lupinus polyphyllus	- Large-leaved lupine
Lupinus pusillus	- Small lupine
Lupinus sericeus	- Silky lupine

-M-

Mangifera indica	- Mango
Medicago sativa	- Alfalfa
Melilotus alba	- White sweet clover
Melitus officinalis	- Yellow sweet clover
Menispermum canadense	- Moonseed
Monstera deliciosa	- Swiss-cheese plant

-N-

| *Narcissus peoticus* | - Narcissus |
| *Narcissus pseudonarcissus* | - Daffodil |

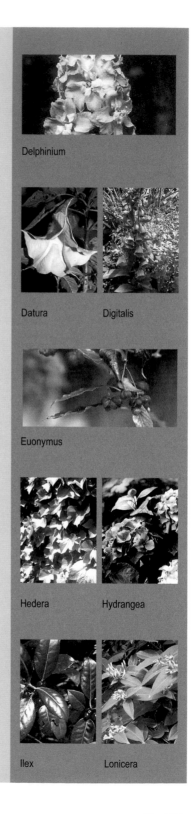

Delphinium

Datura   Digitalis

Euonymus

Hedera   Hydrangea

Ilex   Lonicera

Nerium oleander	- Oleander
Nicotiana tabacum	- Tobacco

-O-

Onoclea sensibilis	- Sensitive fern
Ornithogalum umbellatum	- Star-of-Bethlehem
Oxytropus lambertii	- Purple locoweed

-P-

Papaver nudicaule	- Iceland poppy
Papaver orientale	- Oriental poppy
Papaver somniferum	- Opium poppy
Parthenocissus quinquefolia	- Virginia creeper
Persea americana	- Avocado
Phacelia campanularia	- California canarygrass
Phalaris arundinacea	- Reed canarygrass
Philodendron cordatum	- Philodendron
Phoradendron flavescens	- American mistletoe
Physalis alkekengi	- Chinese-lantern
Physalis peruviana	- Ground-cherry
Phytolacca american	- Pokeweed
Pinus ponderosa	- Ponderosa pine
Primula obconica	- Primula
Polygonatum multiflorum	- Solomon's seal
Prunus pennsylvanica	- Pin cherry
Ptedidium aquilinum	- Bracken

-Q-

Quercus alba	- White oak
Quercus rubra	- Red oak

-R-

Rananculus bulbosus	- Bulbous buttercup
Raphanus raphanistrum	- Wild radish
Raphanus sativus	- Radish
Rhamnus carthartica	- European buckthorn
Rheum rhaponticum	- Rhubarb
Rhododendron macrophyllum	- California rose-baby
Rhus diversiloba	- Western poison-oak
Rhus radicans	- Poison ivy
Ricinus communis	- Castor-bean
Robinia pseudoacacia	- Black locust
Rudbeckia serotina	- Black-eyed Susan
Rumex acetosa	- Garden sorrel

-S-

Sambucus canadensis	- American elder
Sambucus nigra	- European elder
Sarcobatus vermiculatus	- Greasewood
Scilla siberica	- Siberian scilla
Senecop jacobaea	- Tansy ragwort
Sinapis arvensis	- Wild mustard
Solanum dulcamara	- Climbing nightshade
Solanum nigrum	- Black nightshade
Solanum speudocapsicum	- Jerusalem-cherry

Lupinus

Papaver orientalis

Parthenocissus

Phytolacca

Polygonatum   Rhododendron

Solanum tuberosum	- Potato	
Solidago mollis	- Velvety goldenrod	
Sorghum halepense	- Johnson grass	
Suckleya suckleyana	- Poison suckleya	
Symphoricarpos albus	- Thin-leaved snowberry	
Symphytum asperum	- Prickly comfrey	
Symplocarpus foetidus	- Skunk cabbage	

-T-

Tanacetum vulgare	- Tansy
Taxus canadensis	- Canada yew
Thermopsis rhombifolia	- Golden-bean
Thlaspi arvense	- Stinkweed
Thuja	- Thuja
Trifolium pratense	- Red clover
Trifolium repens	- White clover
Tulipa gesneriana	- Tulip

-U-

Urica dioica	- Stinging nettle

-V-

Veratrum viride	- False hellebore
Viburnum opulus	- Guelder-rose
Vicia sativa	- Common vetch

-W-

Wisteria floribunda	- Japanese wisteria

-X-

Xanthium strumarium	- Cocklebur

-Z-

Zigadenus elegans	- White camas

Ricinus

Sedum spectabile

Thuja

Other dangers

A human walks on two legs and does not always see what can happen at ankle and knee height. You could say that anything that may be dangerous for a crawling baby can also be dangerous for a dog. We will give you a few examples.

Cables

Young dogs like to bite into all sorts of things. Wires from lamps, the computer and other electric appliances can be found everywhere in the house. Hide these as far as possible. You can also buy certain materials to wrap around cables and thus protect them.

Detergents

Although most people do not think of detergents as being immediate hazards for dogs, they contain substances which are toxic for dogs. So it is self-explanatory that you should not let your dog walk over them or spray it with detergents, but danger is still lurking around the corner. Just take simple mopping of the floor, something you will have to do more regularly if you have pets. Whichever cleaning equipment you use, at a certain point the floor is wet while you are working. If the dog walks over the wet floor, it will also get detergent on its paws. If the dog licks its paws dry again it will then still ingest toxic detergent.

Chocolate

Sometimes we think that what we see on television is actually true. In cartoons, but also in some programmes, there is a strange notion of dogs and sweets. Do not be tempted to think that what dogs eat in cartoons is actually the right food for dogs in real life. Chocolate is one of those products that humans enjoy, but which is actually toxic for dogs and cats. Chocolate contains certain substances which their bodies cannot break down. So never feed a dog chocolate and definitely do not let it scavenge around. Luckily, most cats do not like sweet food, but dogs do!

Tips

- Get in touch with the breed association for the address of a reliable breeder.
- Visit a number of breeders before buying a puppy.
- Ask to see the parent dogs' papers. The parents must not have any hereditary abnormalities. The eyes must have been examined for hereditary eye diseases and the hips of the parents must have been checked for Hip Dysplasia.
- Never buy a puppy if you have been unable to see its mother or if you have not seen all papers from both parents.
- Never buy a Bullmastiff on impulse, even if it is love at first sight. A Bullmastiff is not a toy that you can throw away when you do not like it anymore.
- Buy a Bullmastiff only through the breed club.
- You have to be extremely consistent when training your Bullmastiff during the first two or three months.
- A puppy has to be socialised and it has to experience a lot of new impressions. Give it time to cope with these impressions. Never overload you puppy with impressions.
- Feed your puppy moderately. Too much weight is bad for the development of its skeleton.
- The advice that the breeder of your puppy gives you should be followed very well, especially during the first period.
- When you want to change this, please discuss it with the breeder of your dog.
- Let children play only moderately with your young dog. They are not at all allowed to drag your Bullmastiff around.
- In case the dog slips a lot on smooth floors, this is bad for its joints. Please do something to prevent this slipping.
- In the beginning you have to make short walks with your puppy. For each week that the puppy is old, you are allowed to walk one minute. So a puppy that is 10 weeks old can go on a walk of 10 minutes.
- In case you are going to visit somebody, first ask if your Bullmastiff is welcome as well. Do not take your dog with you without asking.
- Never accept from your puppy what you would not accept from an adult dog. No means no.
- Its first trip in a car is a real experience for a puppy; make it a pleasant one.
- Do not add supplements to ready-made foods.
- Never give your Bullmastiff cowhide or buffalo hide chews, as they can cause suffocation.
- Do not let your Bullmastiff climb up stairs for the first six months.
- Join a puppy training course with your puppy. It teaches both dog and owner a lot. Especially with a big dog it is extra important that it behaves very well.
- Take care that your dog does not get too fat. Not too much food and plenty of exercise are golden rules.
- Never leave a dog alone with small children.
- Never let your puppy run endlessly after a ball or stick.
- Do not just fight the fleas, but the larvae too.
- Organise a holiday home or a dog-sitter for your Bullmastiff well in advance.
- Taking your dog with you on holiday? It is the best thing you can do. However, make sure that your Bullmastiff will be welcome before you go.
- Allow your Bullmastiff to rest after meals.
- A puppy will mean a lot of work, and sometimes a few grey hairs.
- Good grooming is important for your dog's health.
- Even if the Bullmastiff is an affectionate dog, a rigorous upbringing is important.

Internet

A great deal of information can be found on the internet. A selection of websites with interesting details and links to other sites and pages is listed here. Sometimes pages move to another site or address. You can find more sites by using the available search engines.

For Great Britain

www.the-kennel-club.org.uk
The Kennel Club's primary objective is to promote, in every way, the general improvement of dogs. This site aims to provide you with information you may need to be a responsible pet owner and to help you keep your dog happy, safe and content.

www.bullmastiffassociation.co.uk
The Bullmastiff Association is a UK Breed Club and was founded 1934.

www.britishbullmastiffleague.com
The British Bullmastiff League is a UK Breed Club and it was formed in 1925. It was then called "The Midland Bull And Mastiff Club". As the breed progressed the name was changed to the "British Bullmastiff League" to reflect a National basis as this was the only club that promoted the Bullmastiff as a pure breed at that time.

www.southernbullmastiffsociety.co.uk
The Southern Bullmastiff Society was founded in 1935 with the objective to encourage and promote the breeding and training of the Bullmastiff and to urge the adoption of the breed standard by all breeders and judges.
Part of the Southern Bullmastiff Society is The Southern Bullmastiff Society Welfare, a not-for-profit organisation, which was started in 1988 to find good homes for unwanted Bullmastiffs. The organisation is entirely run by volunteers.
The aims of the organisation are to:
* Rescue abandoned, unwanted or neglected bullmastiffs
* Provide all necessary care, treatment and rehabilitation where possible
* Assess these dogs for adoption and find suitable homes for them

www.bullmastiffsocietyofscotland.com
Here you can find all news about the Bullmastiff in Scotland.

www.welshandwestbullmastiffsociety.co.uk
This Bullmastiff breed club is a UK Breed Club, which was accepted by the Kennel Club and by June 1946 a full committee had been formed with Captain J. Petersen as President.

www.bullmastiffrescueandadoption.co.uk
OUR MISSION STATEMENT.
We rescue abandoned, neglected and surrendered Bullmastiffs. Our aim is to facilitate the re-homing of these dogs into loving forever homes, we do this not for wealth, politics or recognition, but simply because we have a real passion for this wonderful breed.

www.canineinfo.free-online.co.uk
A canine information directory with results service.
This service is provided with our compliments at no cost to the Society or to the Exhibitor

www.canineinfo.idps.co.uk
On this site you can find all Championship Show Results.

www.champdogs.co.uk
Search the champ dogs database for kennels, stud dogs and litters.

www.crufts.org.uk
With over 22,000 happy, healthy dogs enjoying the thrills and excitement of Best In Show with their owners, there's no better place than Crufts to experience and learn about the wonderful world of dogs.

www.discoverdogs.org.uk
Discover Dogs is all about dogs, featuring information about choice, care and training of all breeds of dogs and puppies.

www.doggenetichealth.org
Your one stop resource for practical information and to learn about dog genetic health. A guide for dogbreeders and owners, brought to you by The Kennel Club.

www.dogtraining.co.uk
Your central resource for dog-training, boarding kennels and vets in the UK.

www.fossedata.co.uk
Fosse Data Systems - your first choice for show schedules and catalogues. With the latest show results.
They provide a reliable and professional printing service for shows large and small. Newsletters and yearbooks a speciality.

www.highampress.co.uk
Championship show results & information ~ Show Printing ~ Web Design

www.k9-care.co.uk
The Self-Help site for dog owners. A beautiful website with tons of information on dogs. All you need to know about grooming, training, health care, buying a dog, travel and much more.

www.k9magazine.com
This refreshing magazine is produced with today's conscientious dog owner in mind and provides a fascinating insight into the latest news, views and gossip from the UK and world dog scene as well as an easy access point to valuable advice, tips and expert opinion from some of the pet world's leading authorities.

www.mypetstop.com
An international, multilingual website with information on keeping, breeding, behaviour, health-related issues and much more.

www.pethealthcare.co.uk
At pethealthcare.co.uk they believe that a healthy pet is a happy pet. Which is why they have brought together leading experts to create a comprehensive online source of pet care information.

www.pet-insurance-uk.me.uk
Find low cost pet insurance via this UK pet insurance directory.

www.petlibrary.co.uk
The Golf Help site for dog owners. A beautiful website with tons of information on dogs. All you need to know about grooming, training, health care, buying a dog, travel and much more.

www.rspca.org.uk
The Royal Society for the Prevention of Cruelty to Animals. If you are interested in re-homing a dog (or other animal), pay a visit to your local RSPCA animal centre. This site provides information on animal care.

www.waltham.com
Waltham is a firm specialized in pet care and nutrition. On this website you can find more information on pet care, training and diets.

www.aboutpets.info
The website of the publisher of the About Pets book series. An overview of the titles, availability in which languages and where in the world the books are sold.

For U.S.A.

www.akc.org
The American Kennel Club provides coverage on all accepted breeds. Gives information on registration, pedigrees and dog shows. Look at the website! So much to see about breeders, breeds, registration, addresses and events.

www.bullmastiff.us
This is the website from the American Bullmastiff Association Inc. and this is interesting for bullmastiff fanciers, bullmastiff breeders, bullmastiff exhibitors, bullmastiff owners and all who love this great breed. Within this breeding club you can find a lot of regional breeding clubs.

www.aboutpets.info
The website of the publisher of the About Pets book series. An overview of the titles, availability in which languages and where in the world the books are sold.

Addresses

Becoming a member of a breed association or club can be very useful for good advice and interesting activities. A Bullmastiff club will give you the opportunity to meet other Bullmastiff lovers. Contact The Kennel Club in case addresses or telephone numbers have changed.

The Kennel Club
1 – 5 Clarges Street
Picadilly
London WIJ 8AB
www.thekennelclub.org.uk

Scottish Kennel Club
Eskmills Park Station Road Musselburgh
Edinburgh EH21 7PQ
www.scottishkennelclub.org
E-mail: info@scottishkennelclub.org

The Irish Kennel Club LTD
Fottrell House
Harolds X Bridge,
Dublin 6W
Ireland
www.ikc.ie
E-mail: ikenclub@indigo.ie

Bullmastiff Breed Clubs
The Bullmastiff Association
Sec. mrs Jan Webster
31 Chaucer Drive - The Country Park
Liverpool - L12 0LH
www.bullmastiffassociation.co.uk
E-mail: evenstardavid@aol.com

The British Bullmastiff League
Sec. mrs Samanth Aston
Staffordshire
www.britishbullmastiffleague.com
E-mail:astonpridebullmastiffs@ntlworld.com

The Northern Bullmastiff Club
Sec. mrs D. Massey,
47 School Road South - Killingholme,
Immingham
N Lincs - DN40 3HS
www.northernbullmastiffclub.co.uk
No E-mail yet

The Southern Bullmastiff Society
Sec. Mr B. Blunden,
Evesdrop - Epping Road,
Broadley Common - Nazeing,
Essex - EN9 2DH
www.southernbullmastiffsociety.co.uk
No E-mail yet

The Bullmastiff Society Of Scotland
Sec. Leigh Thomson
www.bullmastiffsocietyofscotland.com
E-mail: leigh4braeaaron@blueyonder.co.uk

The Welsh And West Of England Bullmastiff Society
Sec. dr. Ronald W. James
Holmeswood - Main Street
Old Weston
Cambridgeshire - PE28 5LL
www.welshandwestbullmastiffsociety.co.uk
E-mail: r.w.james@talk21.com

The American Kennel Club
www.akc.org
United Kennel Club
The United Kennel Club was established in 1998. It is the largest all-breed performance-dog registry in the world, registering dogs from all 50 states and 25 foreign countries.

UKC
100 E Kilgore Rd Kalamazoo MI
49002 – 5584
Office hours: 09:00 to 16:30 (E.S.T.)
Monday trough Friday.

Breed Association
American Bullmastiff Association, Inc.
Cco. Lindy Whyte
2061 Henderson Avenue
Washington, PA 15310
www.bullmastiff.us
E-mail: tryumphe@comcast.net

Profile

Name:	Bullmastiff
Group:	Working Group
Origin:	Great Britain
F.C.I. Classification:	Group 2: Pinchers and Schnauzers, Molossers and Swiss mountain dogs Section 2.1
Breed Association established:	The British Bullmastiff League is a UK Breed Club and it was formed in 1925; it was then called "The Midland Bull And Mastiff Club".
First breed standard:	As long ago as 1785, there was written reference to large dogs of the Bullmastiff kind. The Bullmastiff was recognised by the Kennel Club in 1924 as a pure breed. The American Kennel Club recognized the breed in 1933.
Original use:	Gamekeeper's guard; eventually the Bullmastiff was used in other capacities, such as a sentry or guard dog as well as work with the army and police.
Use today:	Trained and socialised the Bullmastiff will make a wonderful family pet and guardian.
Weight:	Bitch: 41 – 49,9 kg (90 - 110 lbs) Dog: 49.9 - 59 kg (110 - 130 lbs)
Height:	Bitch: 61 – 66 cm (24 – 26 ins) Dog: 63.5 – 68.5 cm (25 – 27 ins)
Life expectancy (average):	10 years